BUILD UP YOUR
LEGO HALLOWEEN VILLAGE

by David Younger

HALLOWEEN TRAIN

Copyright © 2020 David Younger

Model designs by David Younger - Cover illustration by Joseph Fells - Layout design by Camilla Lovell

No part of this publication may be reproduced, distributed, or transmitted in any form or by any means without the prior written permission of the publisher. Although every precaution has been taken to verify the accuracy of the information contained herein, no responsibility is assumed for any errors or omissions, and no liability is assumed for damages that may result from the use of this information. Model designs remain the copyright of the designer and cannot be resold.

LEGO, the Brick and Knob configurations, and the Minifigure are trademarks of the LEGO Group, which does not authorize or endorse this book.

www.inklingbricks.com

Contents

HOW TO GET THE BRICKS
Page 2

LOCOMOTIVE
Page 4

PUMPKIN CAR
Page 28

TOXIC TANKER
Page 36

FRANKENSTEIN CAR
Page 50

PLANT CAR
Page 60

SKELETAL STOCK CAR
Page 76

CABOOSE
Page 82

How to get the bricks

Most people's first step for getting all the needed bricks will be their own collection of LEGO bricks! Use the brick lists at the end of each set instructions to find the bricks you already have, and figure out what you still need to get. It's easy to order any bricks you still need.

LEGO.com

Aside from the Pick a Brick walls at the official LEGO Stores, there are two ways LEGO allows you to purchase individual LEGO bricks through their website at **www.LEGO.com**: Pick A Brick and Bricks & Pieces (to find this, click Support then Replacement Parts).

For both services, you can simply type in the part number (shown in the Brick List for each model) to search for it. Please note that LEGO.com's part availability constantly changes depending on which LEGO bricks are being manufactured at the time so not everything might be available.

Bricklink

www.Bricklink.com is a website owned and operated by The LEGO Group which brings together numerous independent sellers from around the world who all run their own stores selling individual LEGO bricks. Buyers can shop for bricks individually, or upload Wanted Lists and use Bricklink's auto-finder to generate a list of stores that you can buy from to get all the bricks you need. You also have the option of buying brand new or used.

Uploading a Wanted List

Rather than having to add every brick to a wanted list individually, Bricklink allows you to upload lists of bricks to generate an entire wanted list in one go. The list for each model can be found at the web address at the beginning of each model's section in this book. Head to that address and then follow these steps:

1. Select all the text and copy it. It should begin with <INVENTORY> and end with </INVENTORY>.

2. Sign into Bricklink.com, hover over Want at the top right, then click Upload.

3. Click Upload BrickLink XML format.

4. In the drop down box next to Add to select Create New Wanted List and type in a name for your new wanted list a name.

5. Right click in the box which says Copy and paste here and click paste to paste in the XML code.

6. Click Proceeed to verify items and then Add to Wanted List at the bottom of the next page.

Your wanted list is now uploaded! Hover over Want at the top right of Bricklink then click Wanted List to see a all of your wanted lists.

Buying bricks with Bricklink

Although you can buy bricks individually, the quickest way to do this is with Bricklink's auto-finder feature:

1. From the Wanted List page, click the name of the Wanted List you'd like to purchase, then click the Buy All button.

2. Set the locations you're willing to purchase from with the Store Location drop down buttons.

3. Click the Auto-select button and then Start. This will create a list of stores that combined have all your needed bricks assigned to it.

4. Check the assigned percentage at the top right. If this is below 100%, some bricks can't be found from the stores specified in your search preferences. You may need to widen the stores you're willing to buy from, search for a used part instead of a new part, or substitute it. To find out which bricks these are, scroll down below the list, and click Wanted Items.

5. If everything looks good, however, click Create carts to add them to your cart, then click Checkout one by one from each store to purchase the bricks you need from each individual seller.

It's very rare that a single store will have all the bricks you need, so you should expect to be buying from multiple sellers – just remember that you'll need to pay postage on each separate store order.

How to keep the price low

Because Bricklink doesn't use set prices, the cost of bricks can vary between sellers. Here are some techniques for getting the cost as low as it can go:

Finding the expensive bricks

When you have your list of stores, before you click Create carts, you can click the Edit button beside each store to see which bricks you're buying from them. In the Sort by drop down box, choose Price and then scroll to the bottom to see which bricks are the most expensive.

Substitutions

One of the best things about LEGO is how versatile it is, so it's easy to swap bricks out for others. If a 1x8 brick is too expensive, for example, try swapping it for two 1x4 bricks – but always check the instructions to ensure a brick isn't structurally important first. Or if a specific color is too expensive, try swapping it for a more available color. You can make these changes on the Wanted List page, then simply run the auto-finder again.

Avoiding expensive stores

If a particular store is too expensive overall, you can exclude it from the auto-finder results. Click the store name to go to its store page, click the Favorite Stores drop-down box at the top, click Bookmark this store, then choose Dislike before clicking Bookmark.

The most common substitutions for train pieces are the wheels and the magnetic couplers. Make sure you price all of them up to find out what will be cheapest for you:

Wheels	Couplers
2878c02	29085c01
38339c01	91994

LOCOMOTIVE

Number of bricks: 313
www.inklingbricks.com/parts/halloweenlocomotive.txt

1

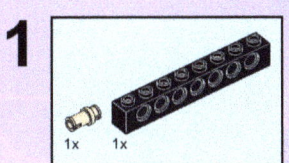

2

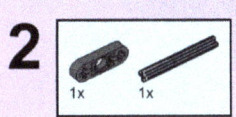

3

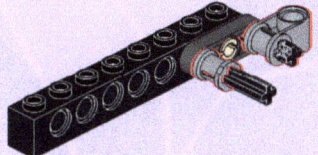

4

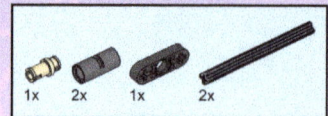
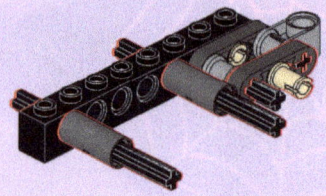

5

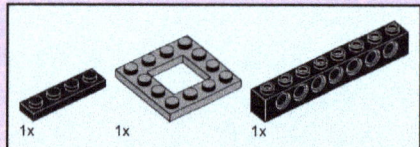
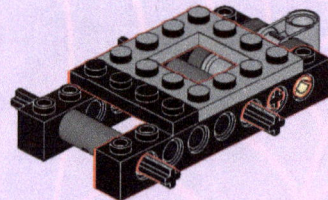

6

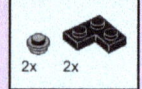
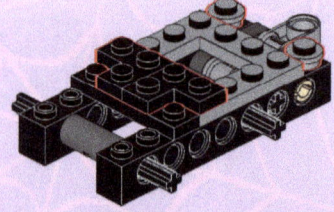

7

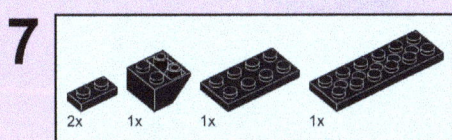

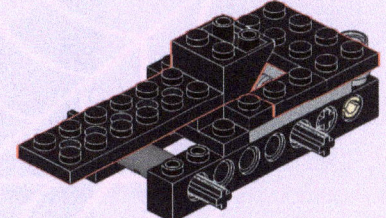

8

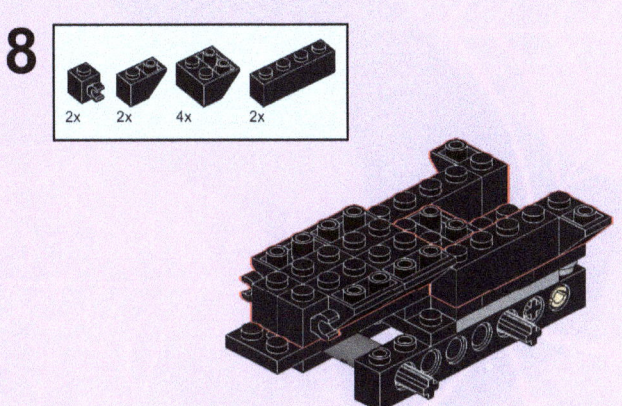

9

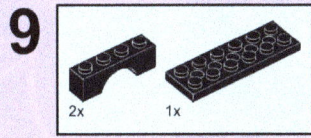

10

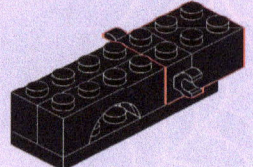

11

12

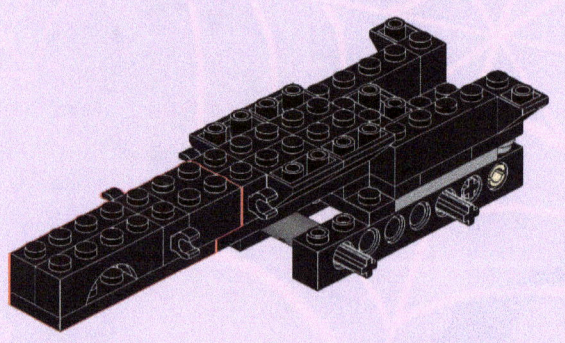

13

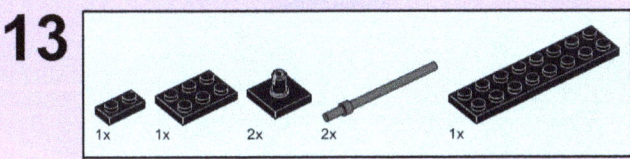

14

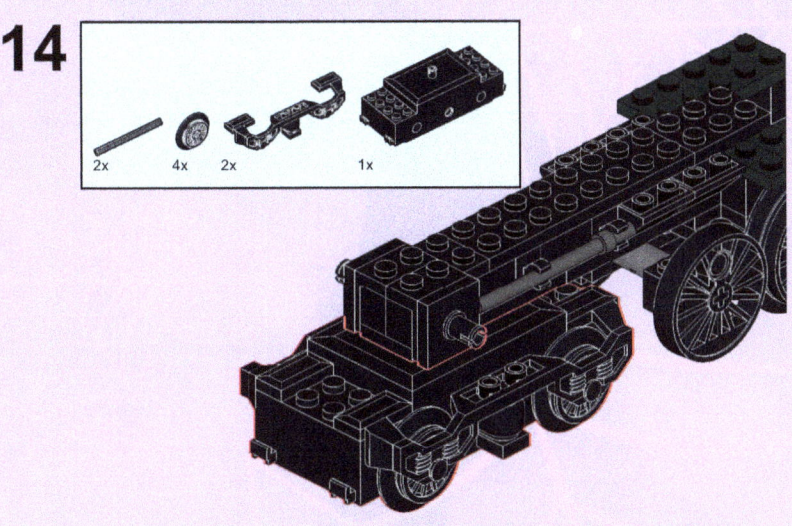

15

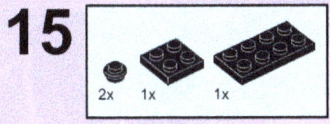

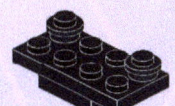

16

17

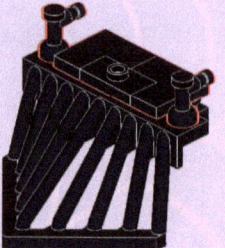

18

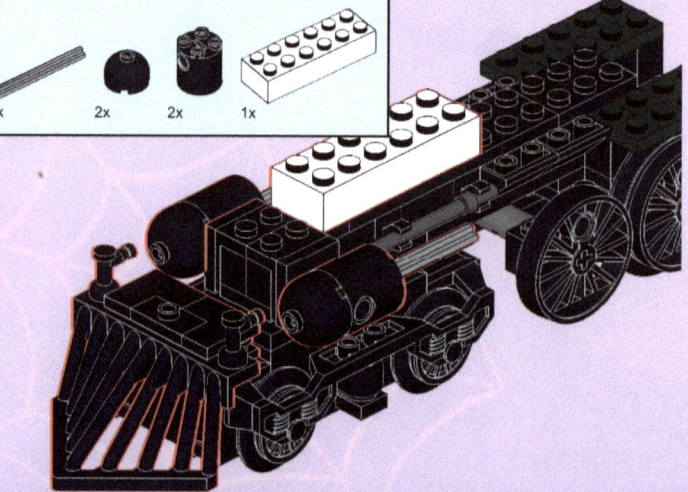

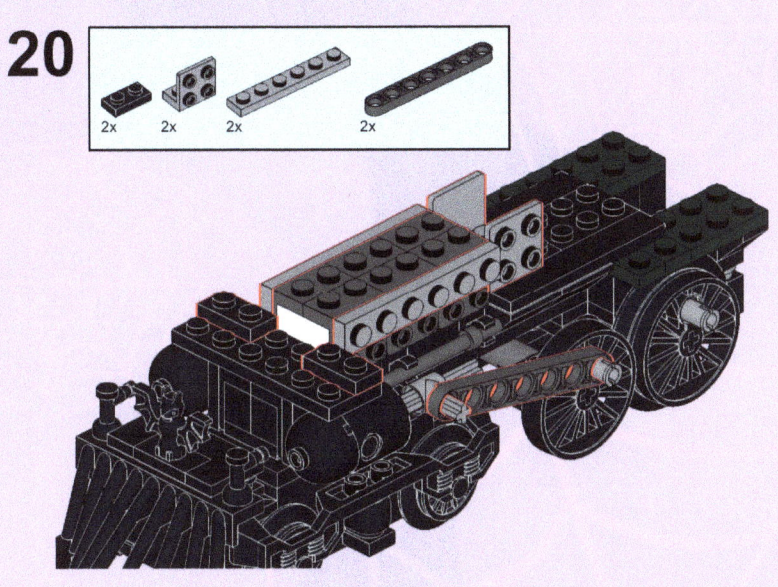
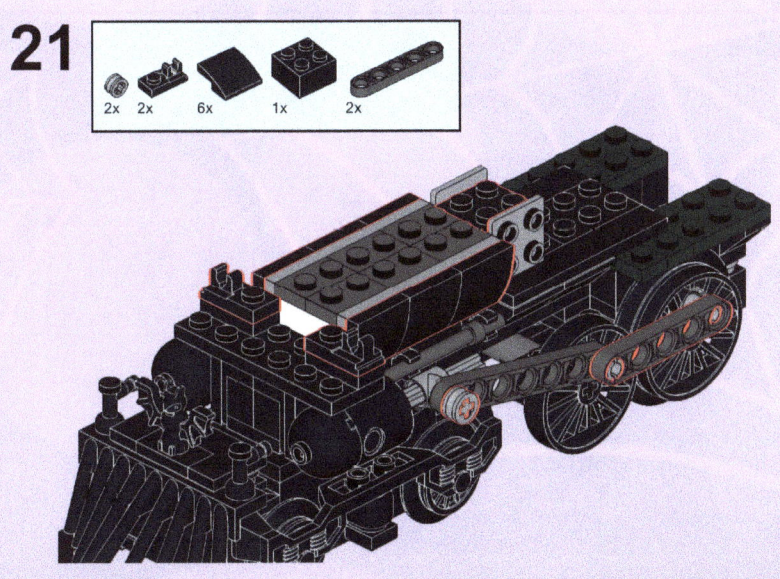

22

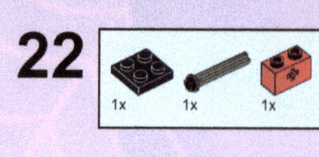

23

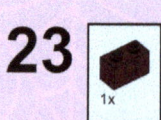

24

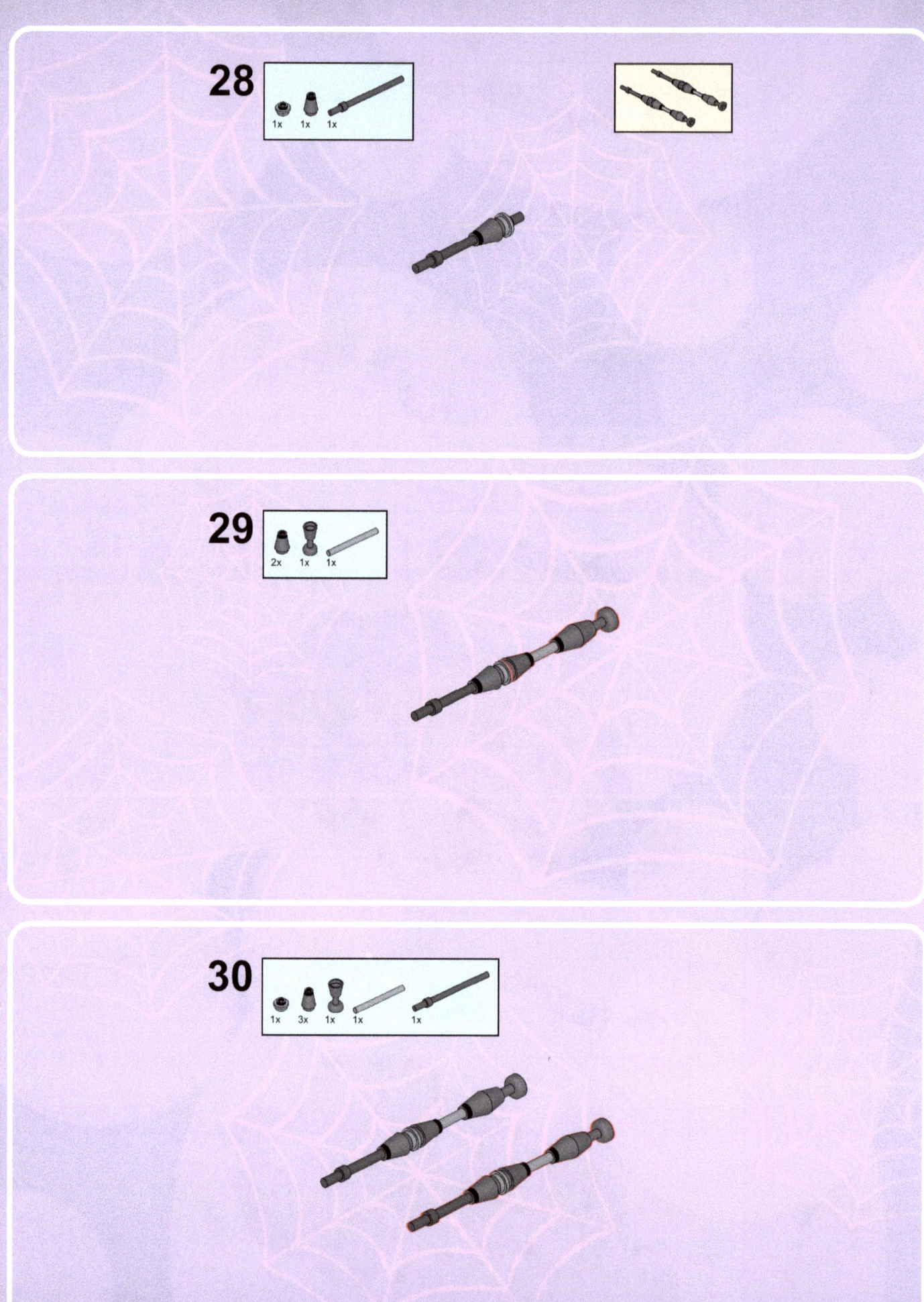

31

32

33

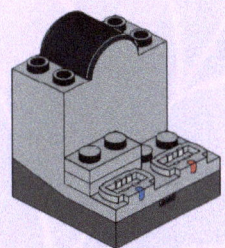

34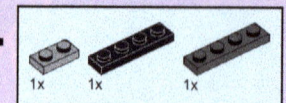

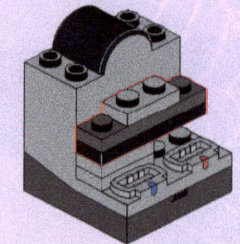

35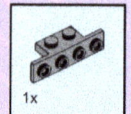

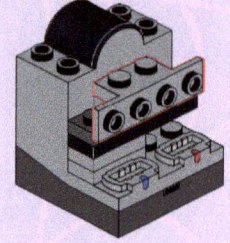

36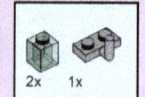

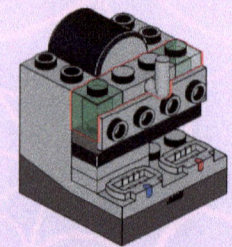

37
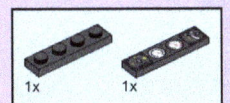
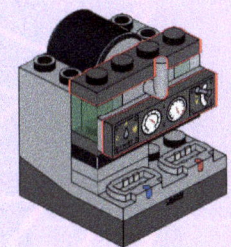

38
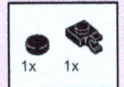

39
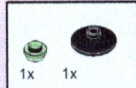

46

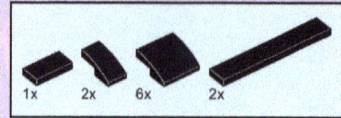

47

48

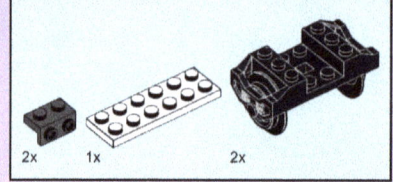

49

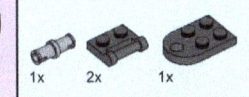

50

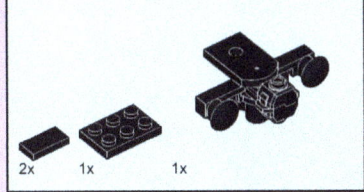

51

52
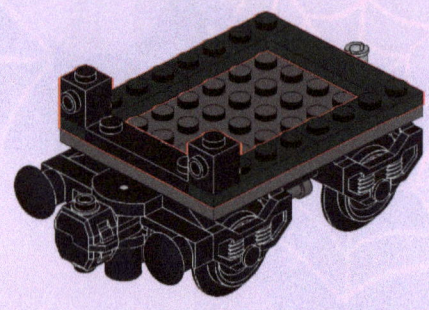

53

54
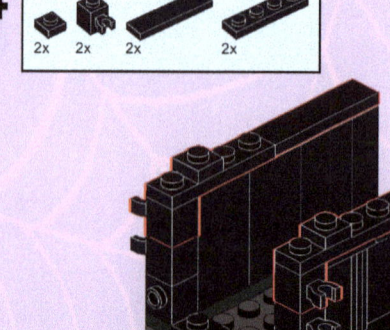

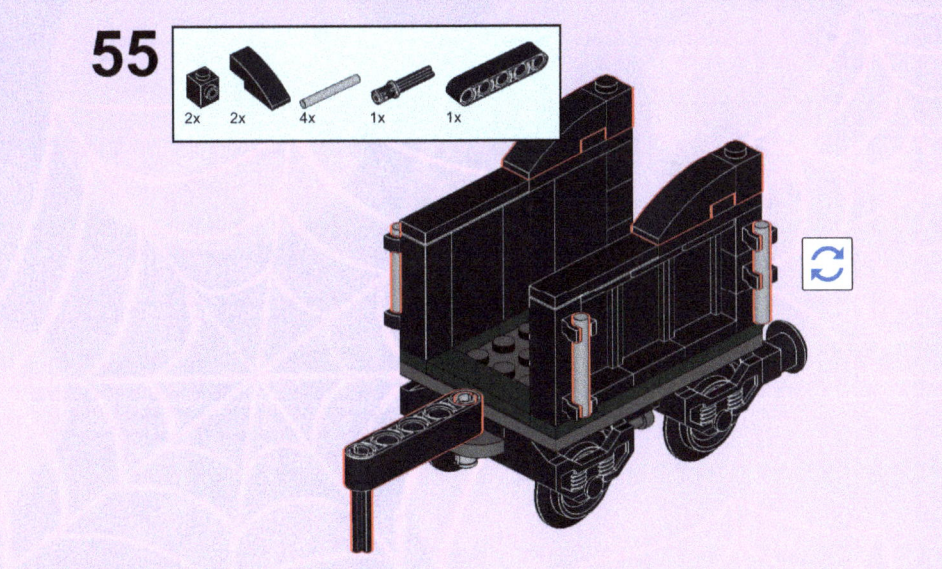

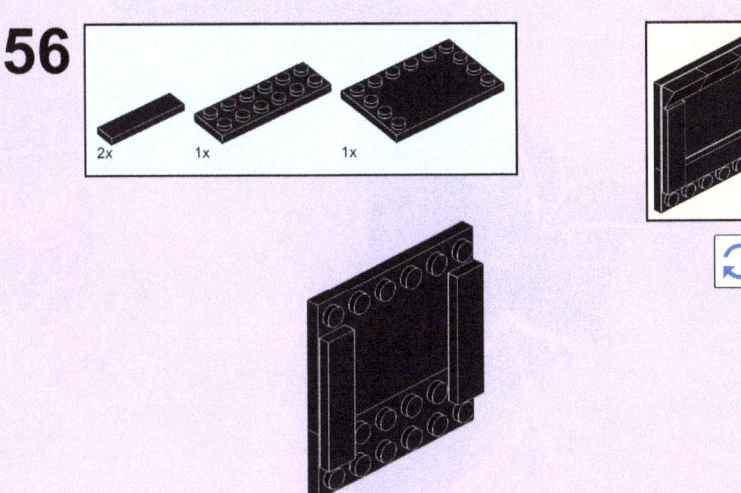

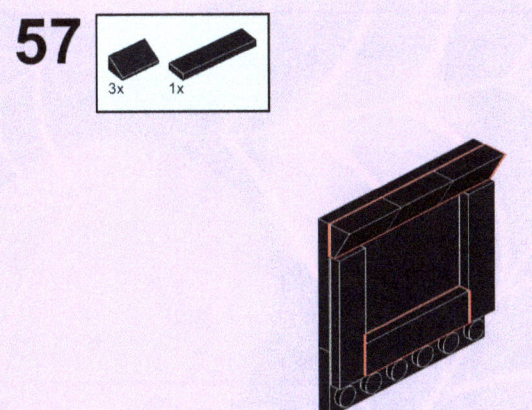

58

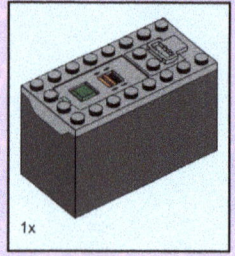

59

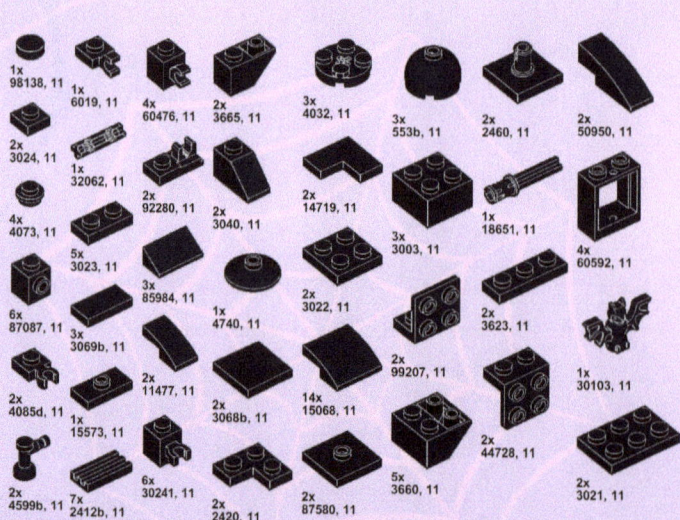

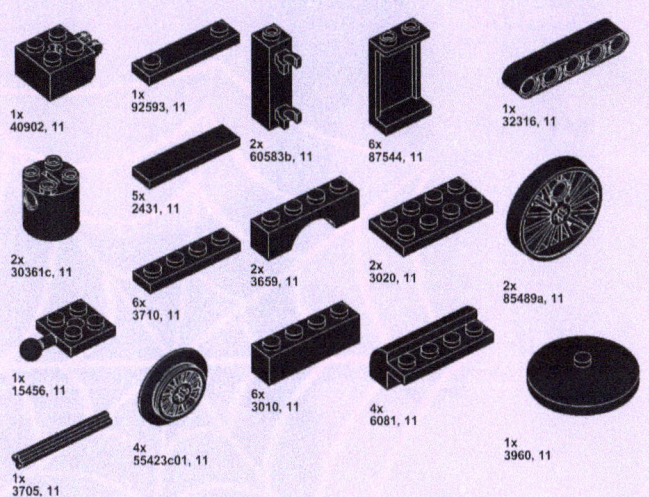
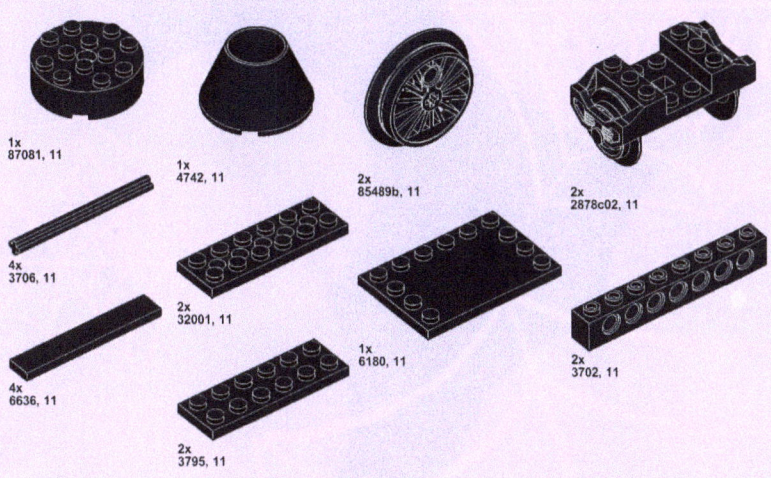
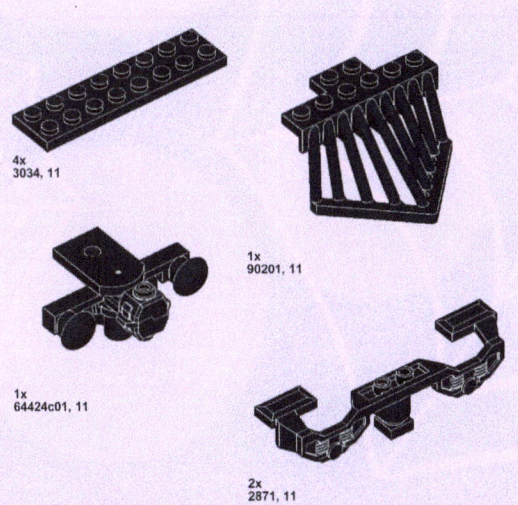

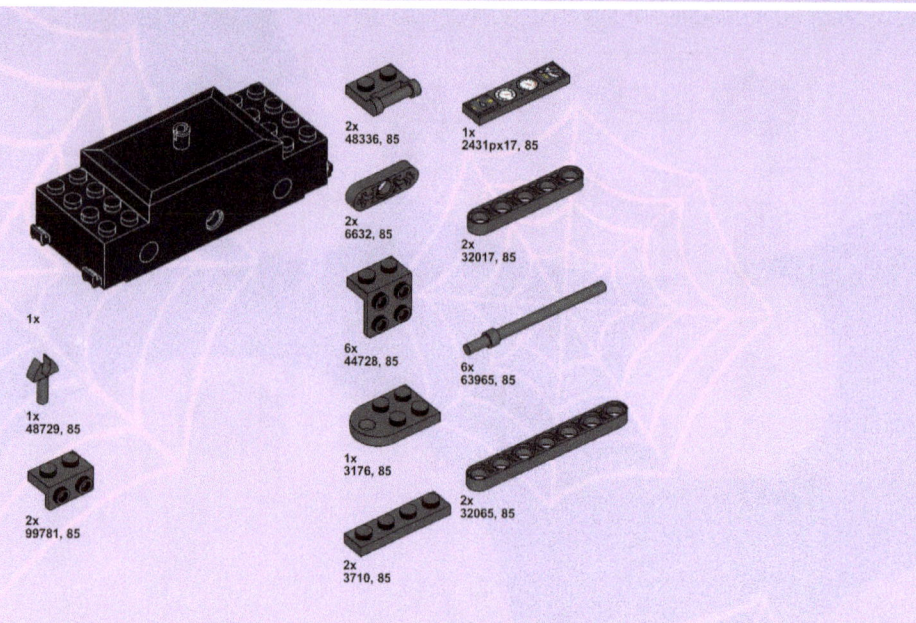
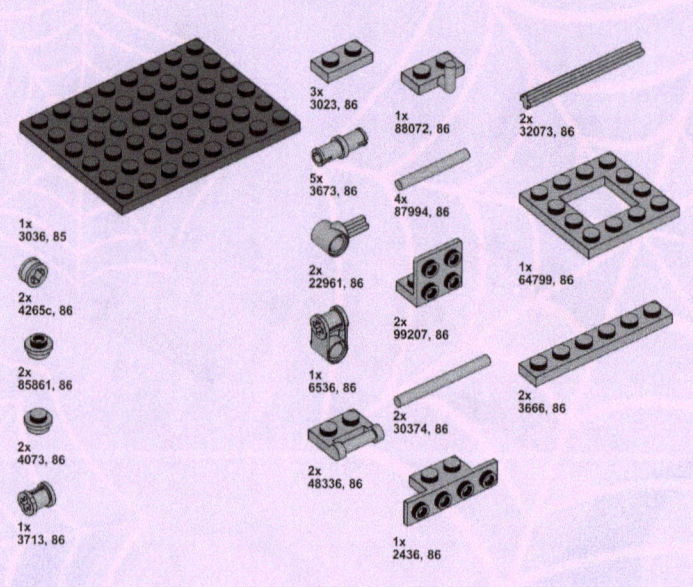
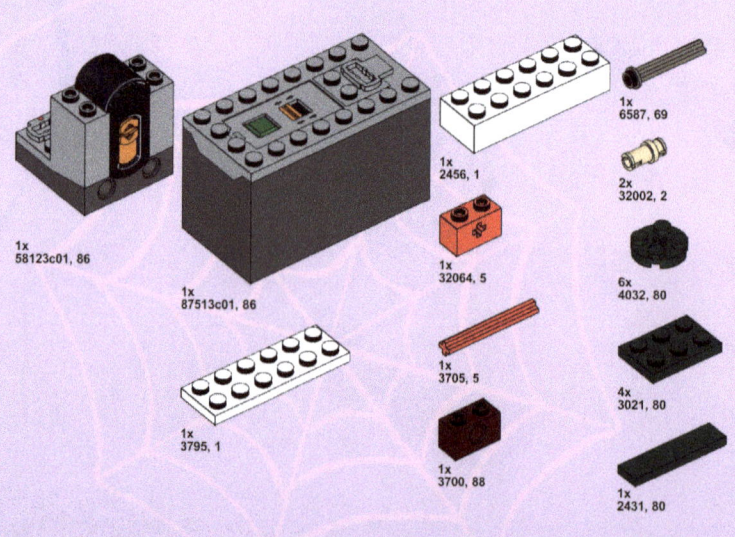

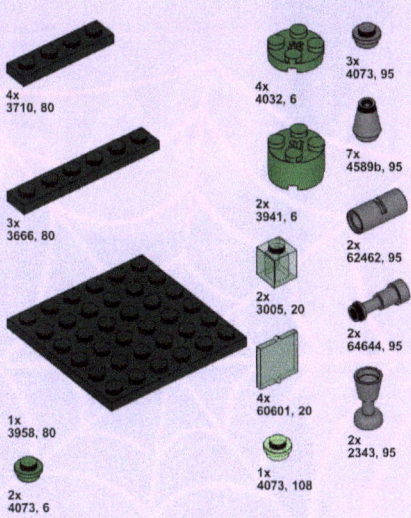

PUMPKIN CAR

Number of bricks: 121
www.inklingbricks.com/parts/pumpkincar.txt

1

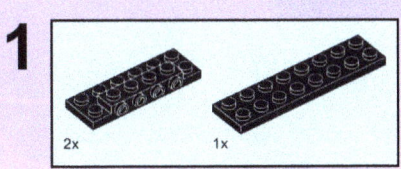

2

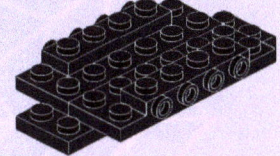

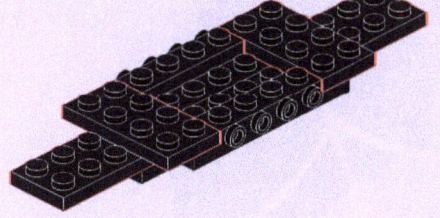

3

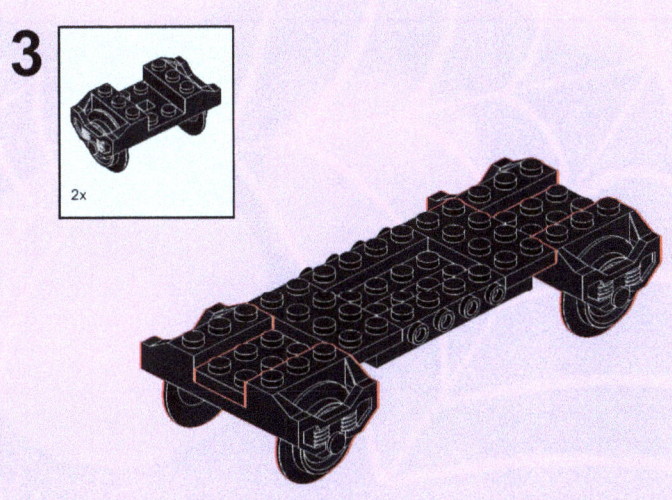

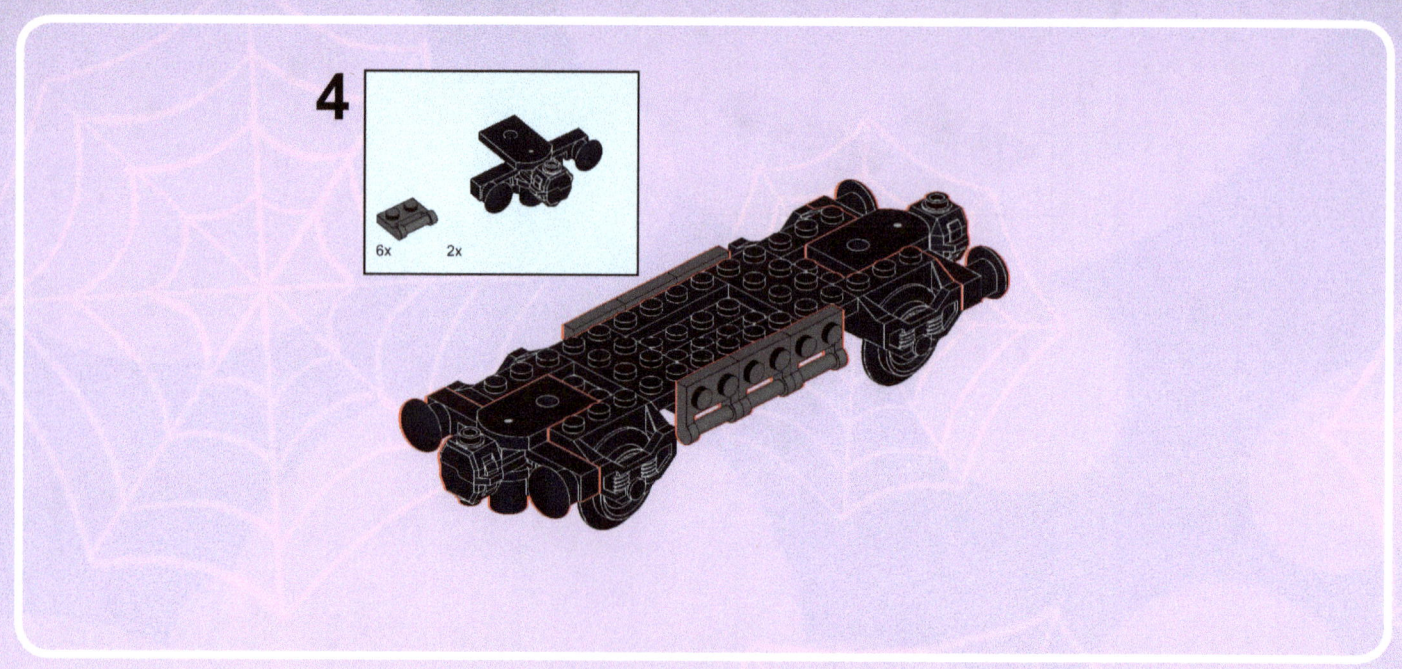
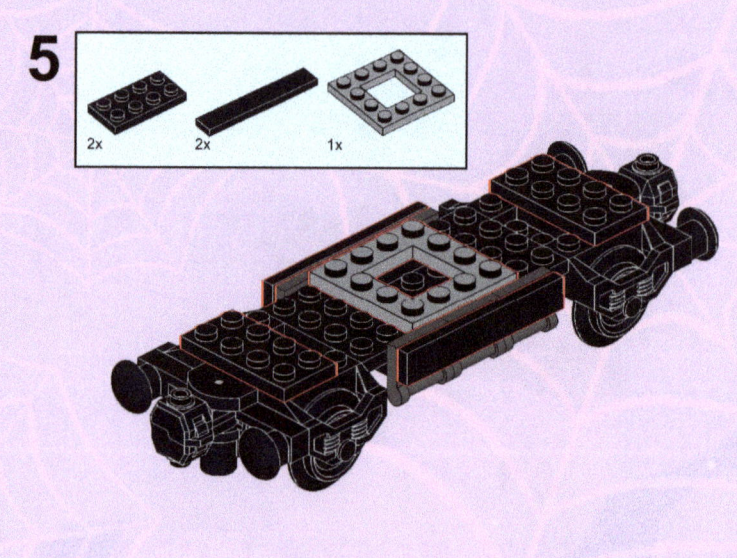

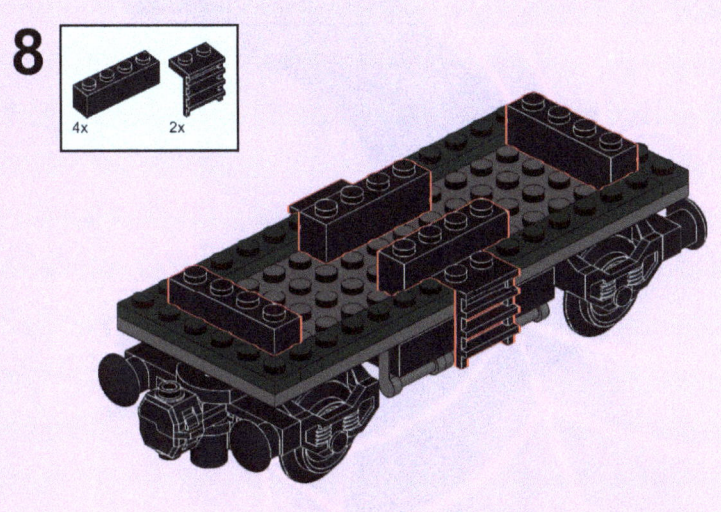

10

11

12

13

14

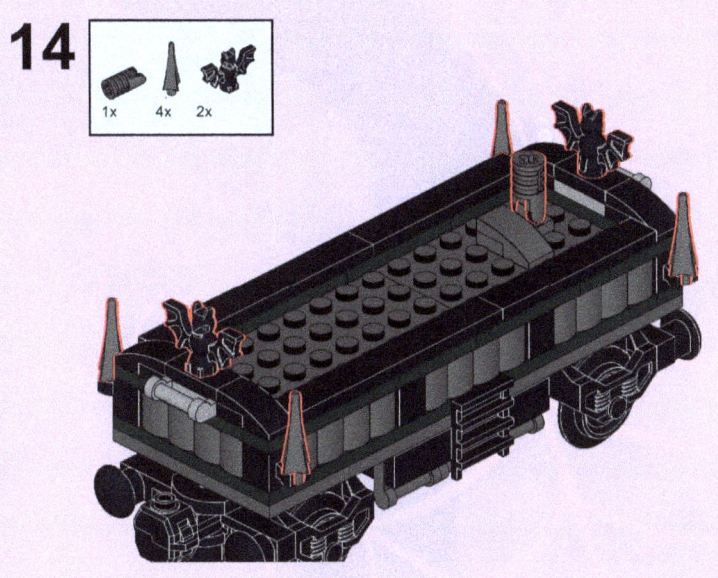

15

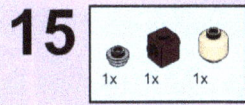

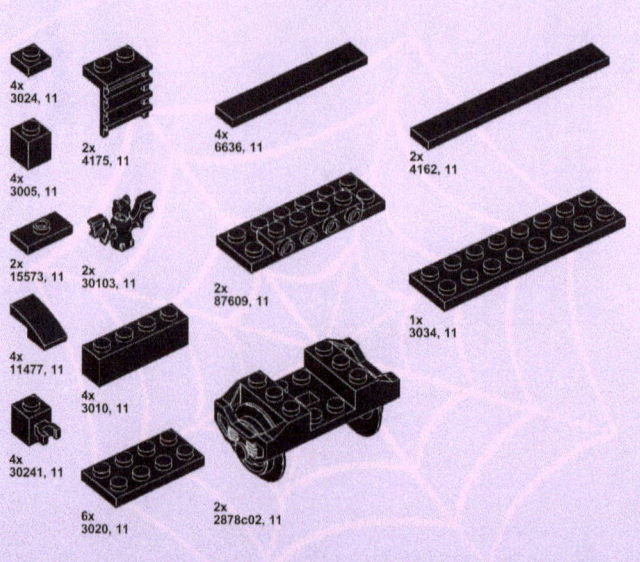

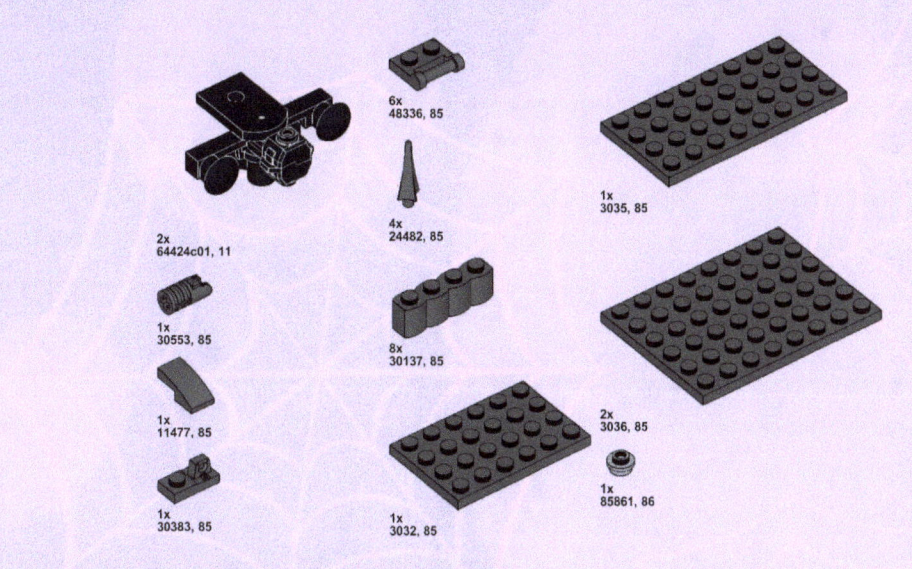
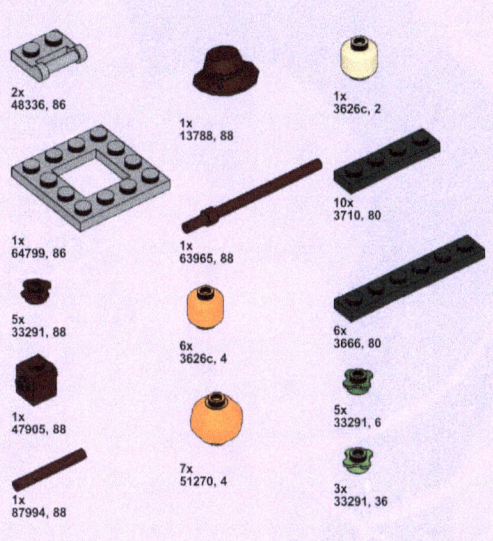

TOXIC TANKER

Number of bricks: 241
www.inklingbricks.com/parts/toxictanker.txt

1

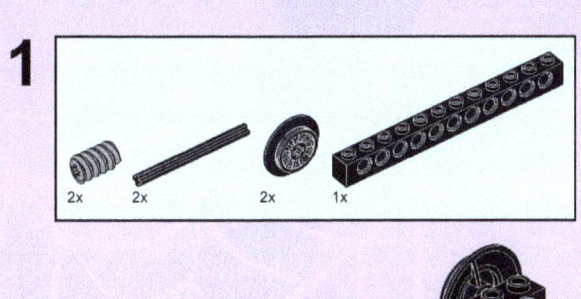
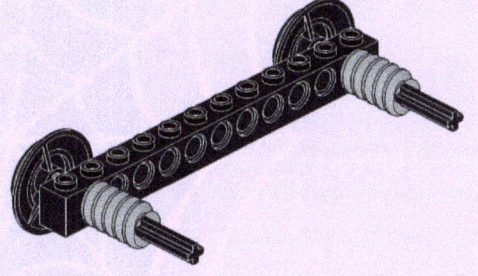

2

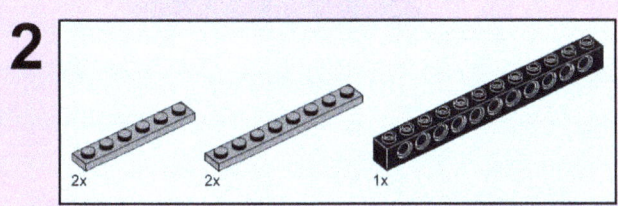
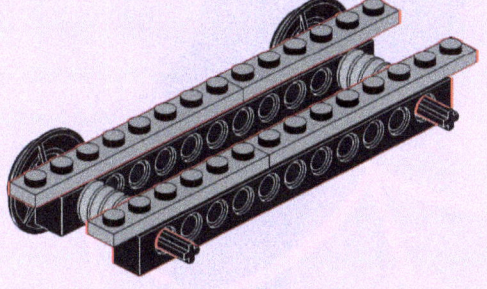

3

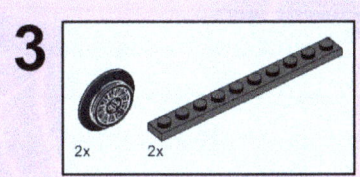
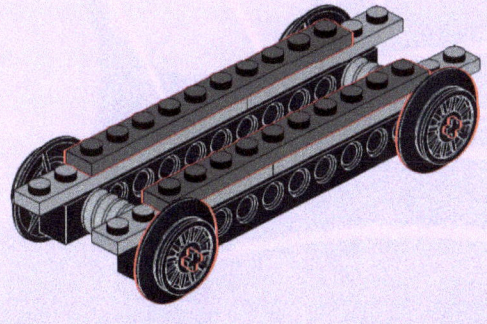

37

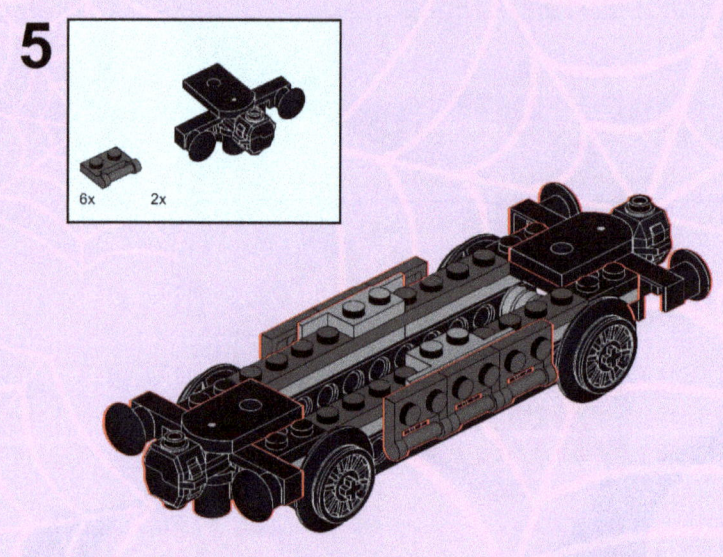
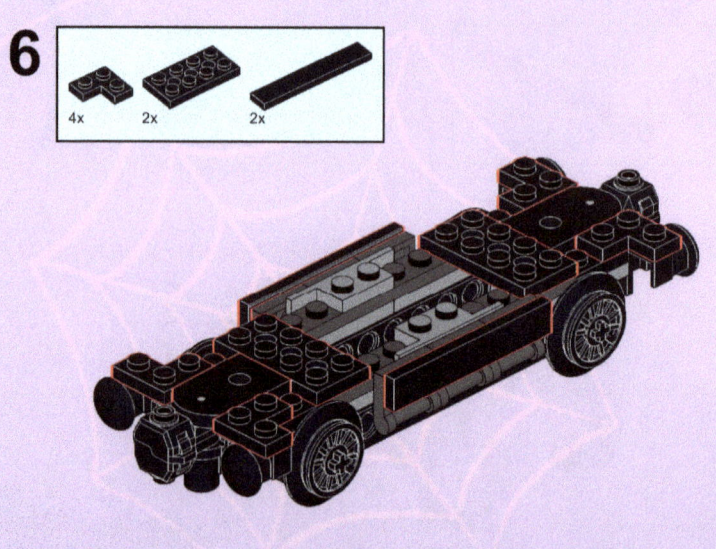

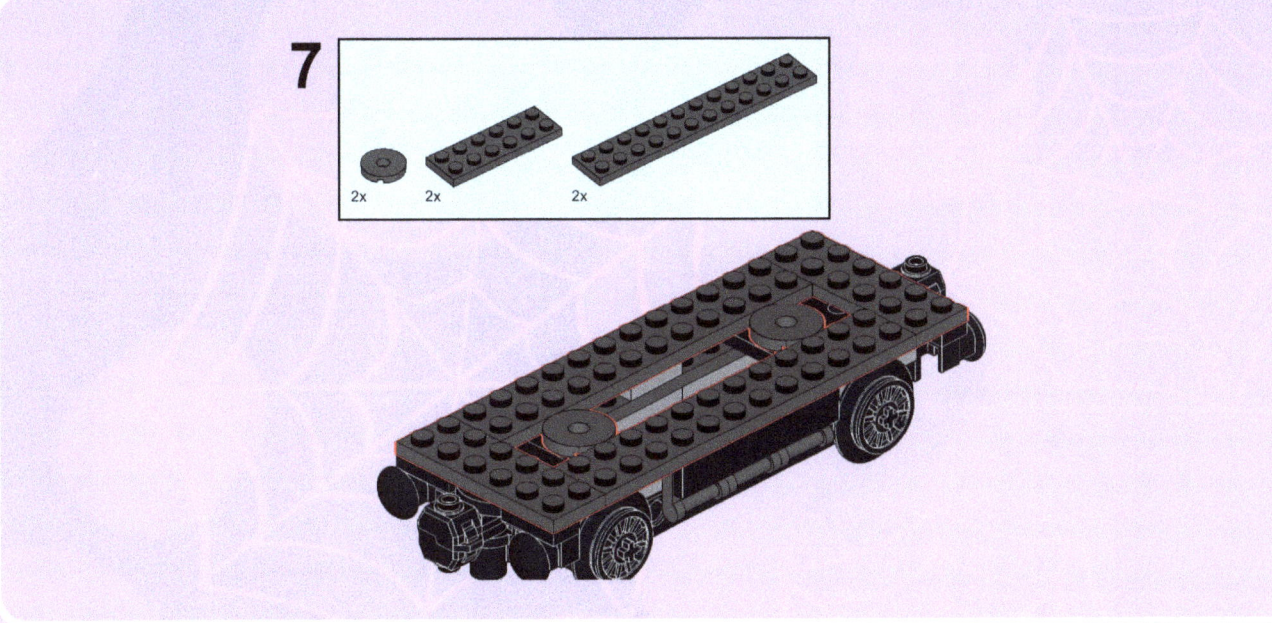

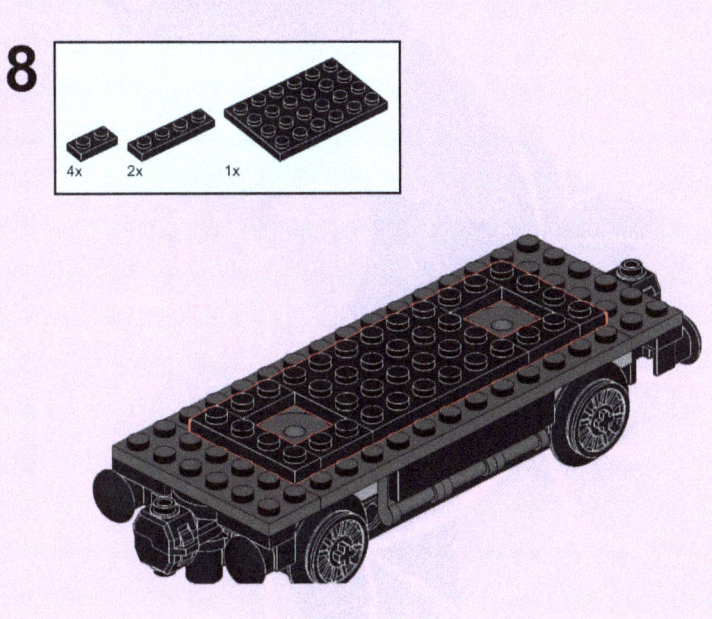

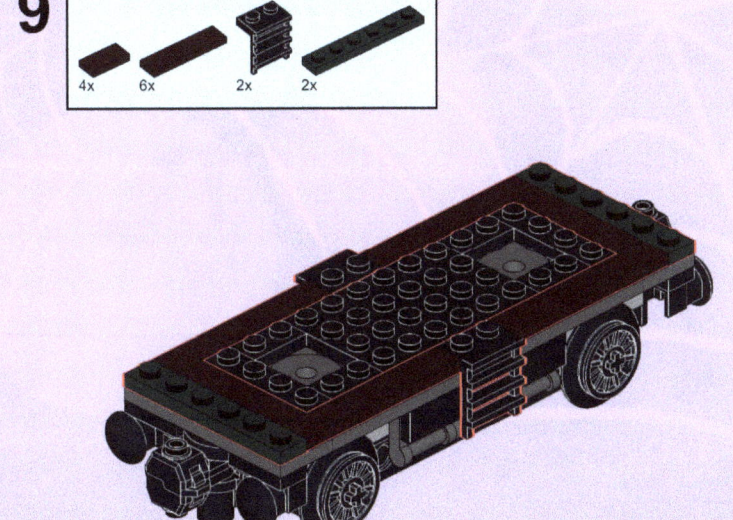

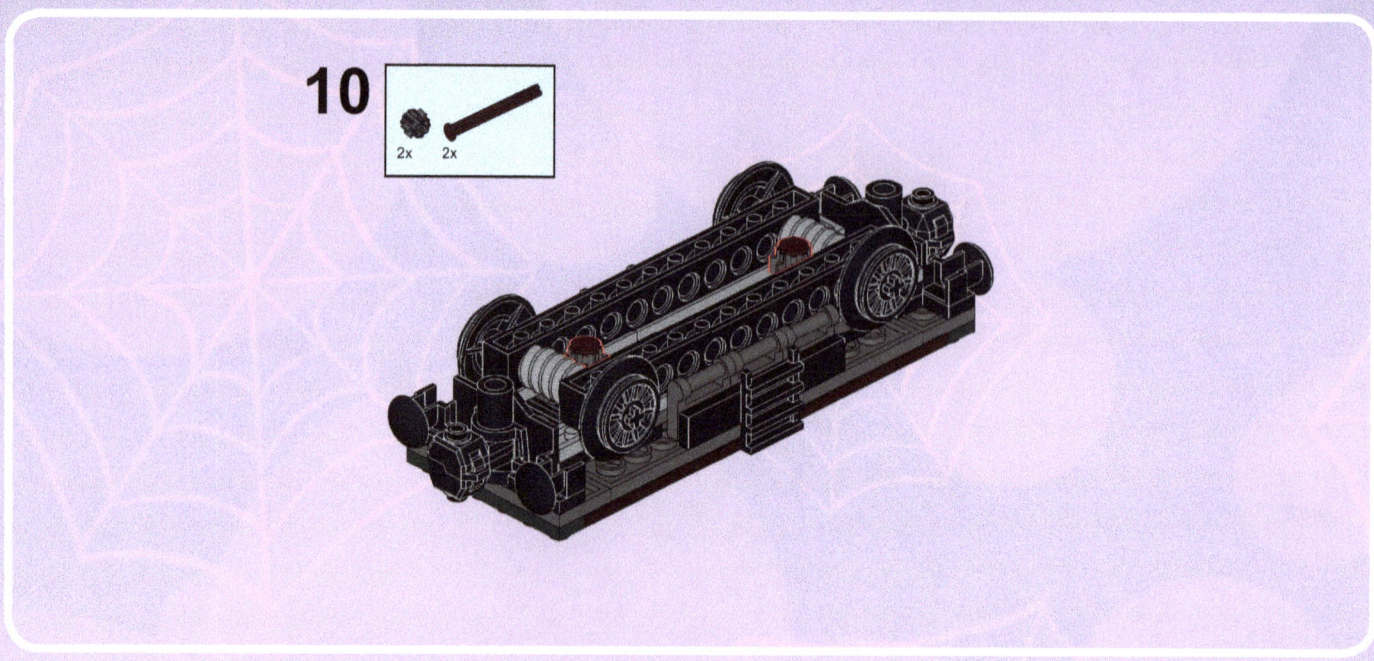

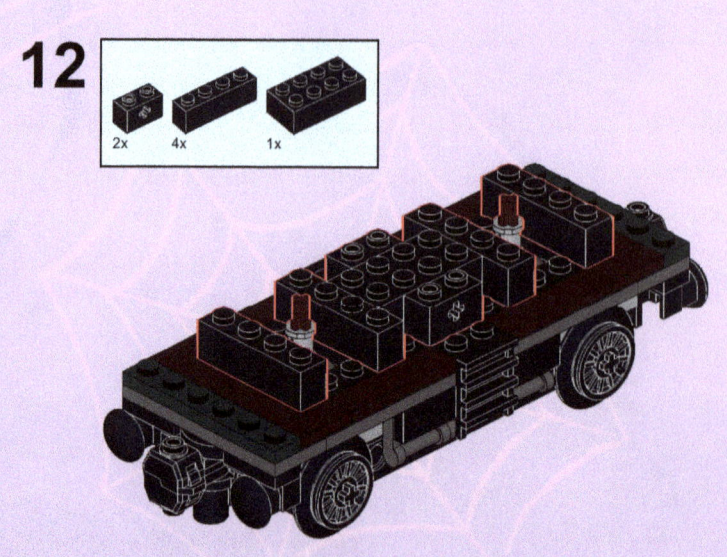

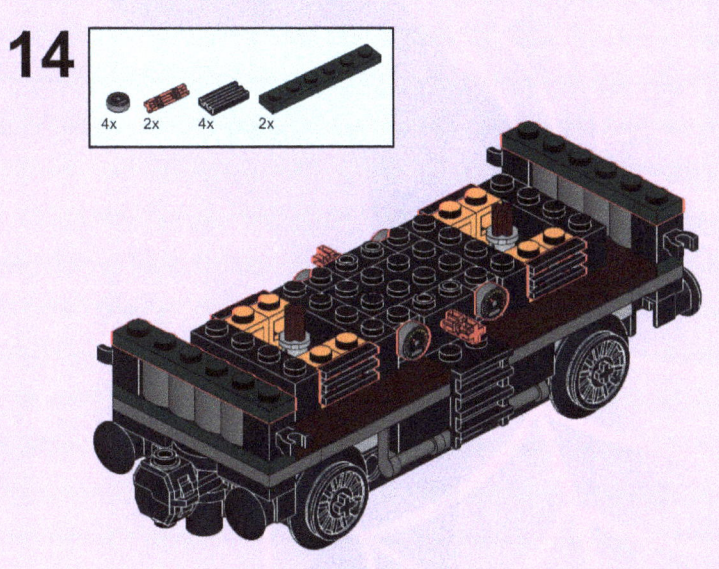

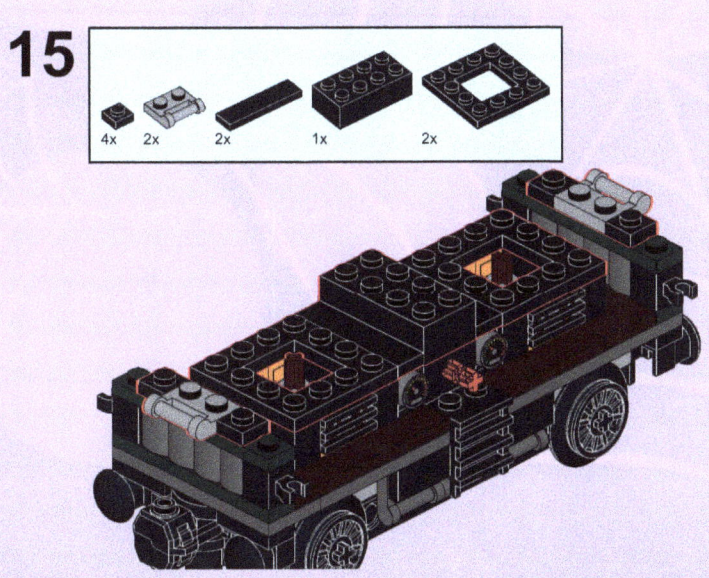

16

17

18

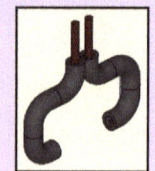

19

20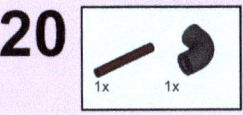

21

22

23 1x

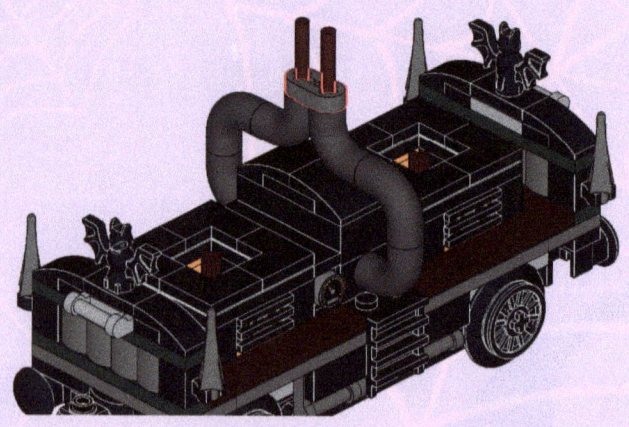

24 2x

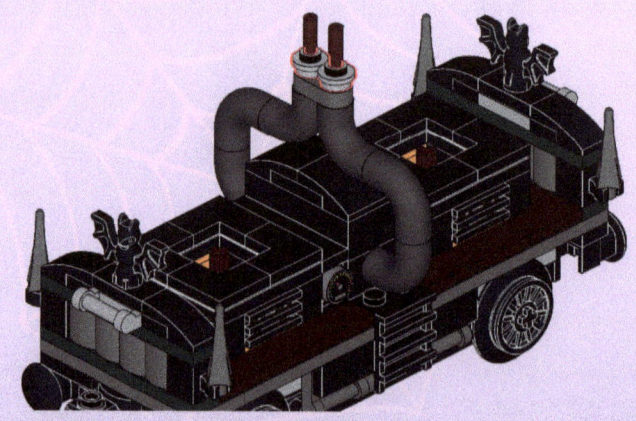

25

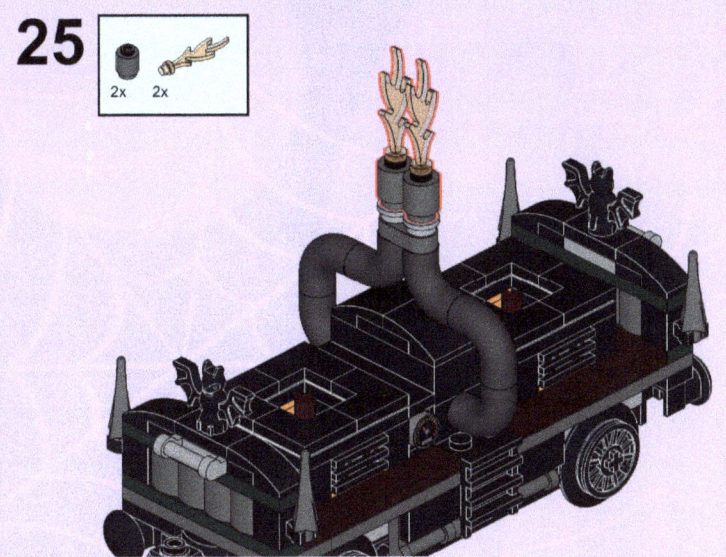

26

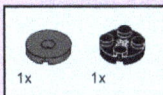 

27

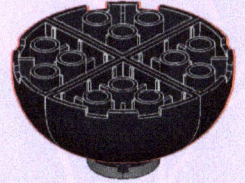

28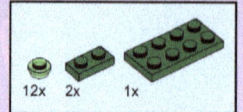

29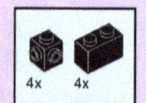

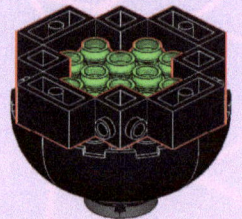

30

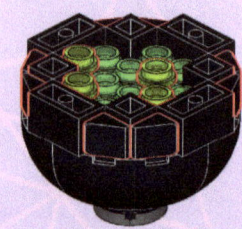

31

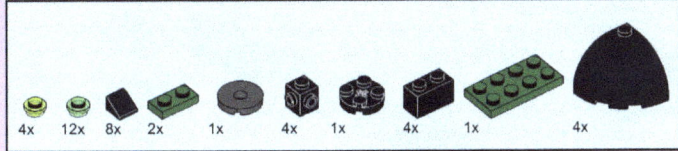

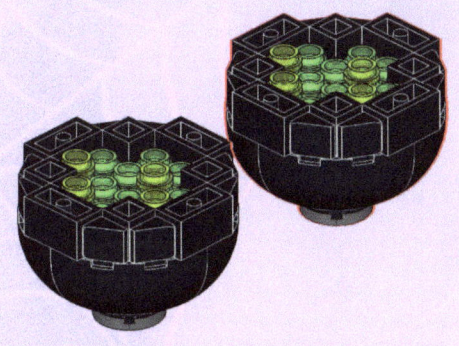

32

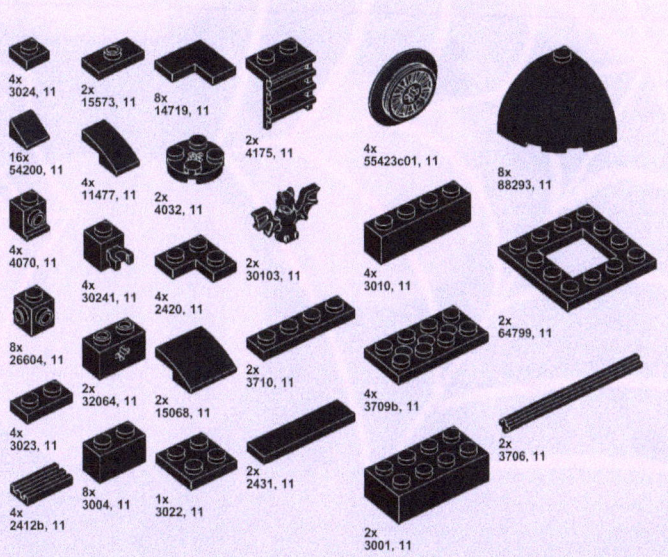

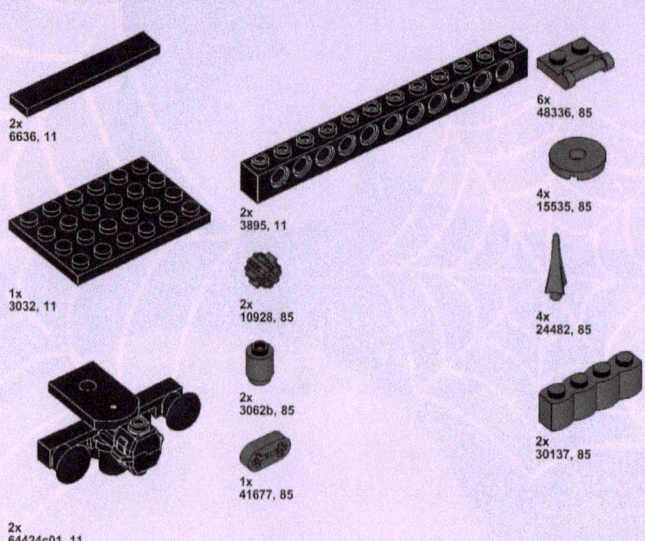
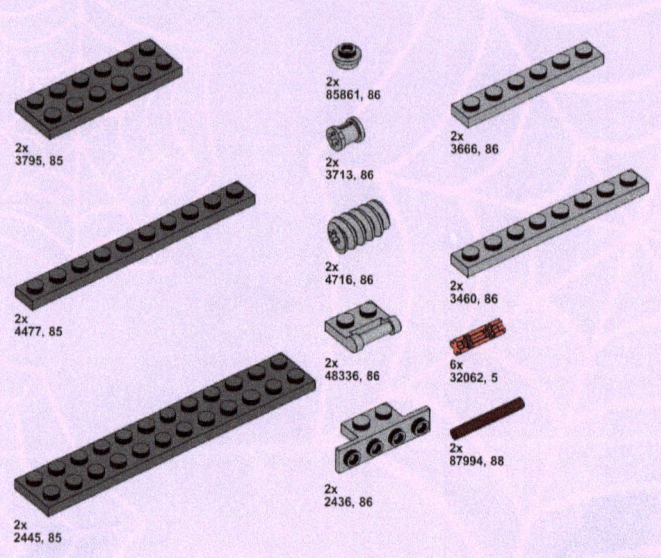
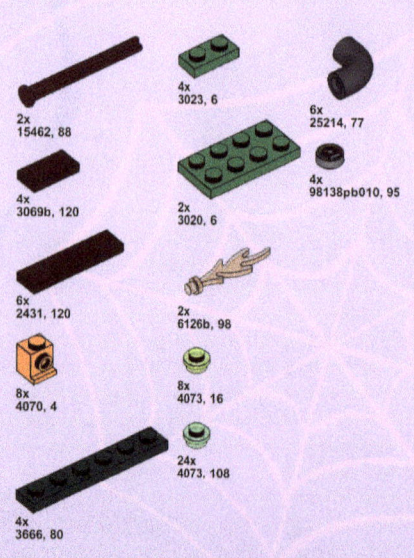

FRANKENSTEIN CAR

Number of bricks: 170

www.inklingbricks.com/parts/frankensteincar.txt

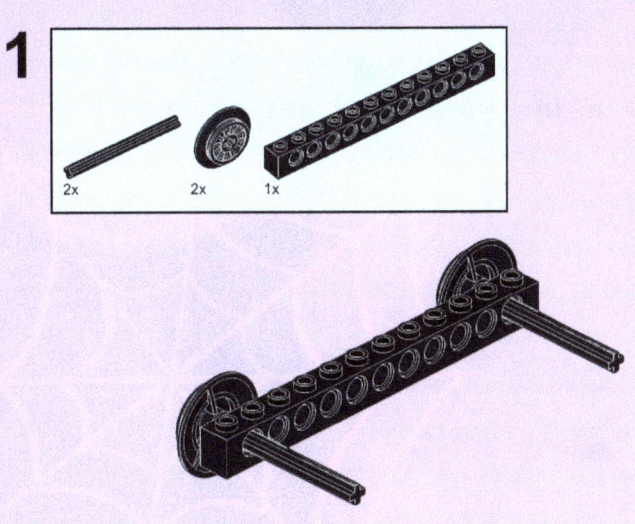

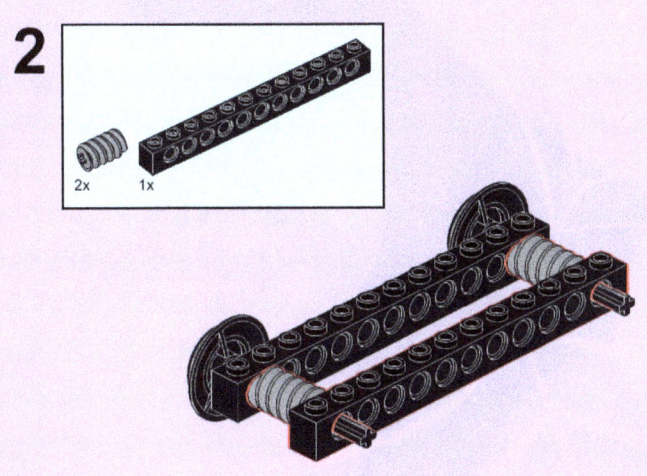

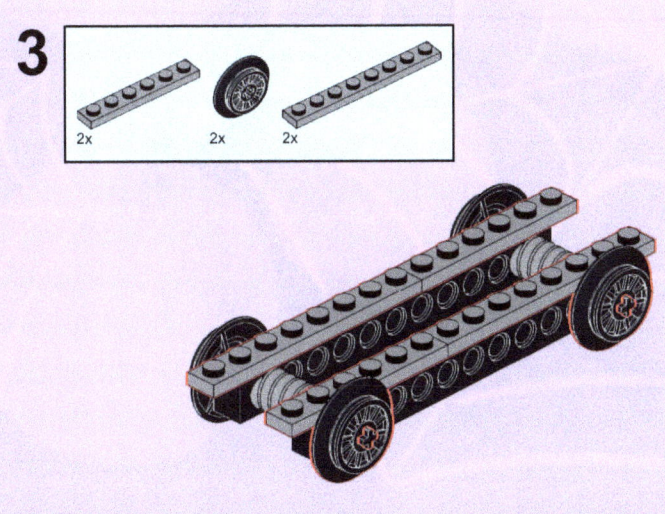

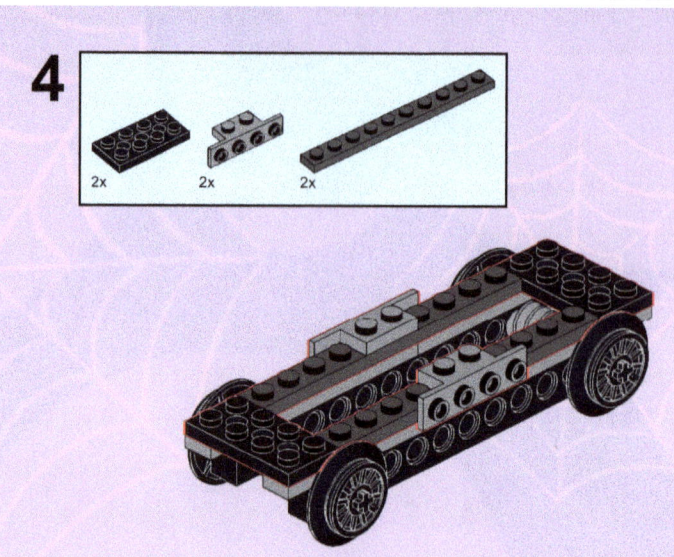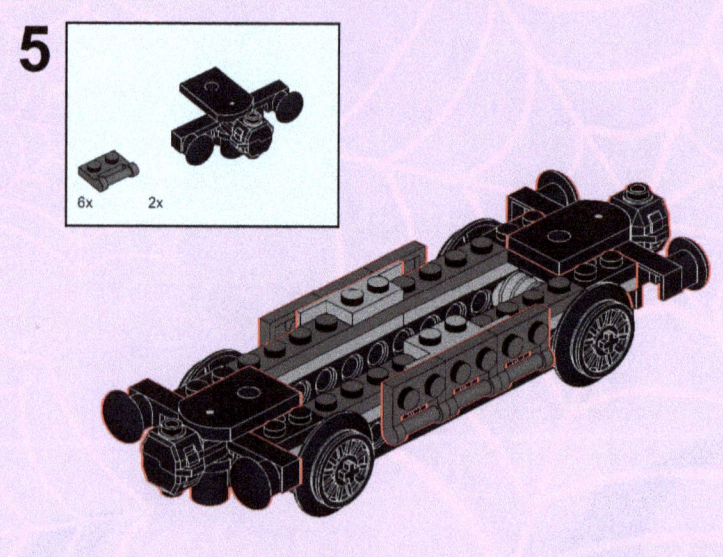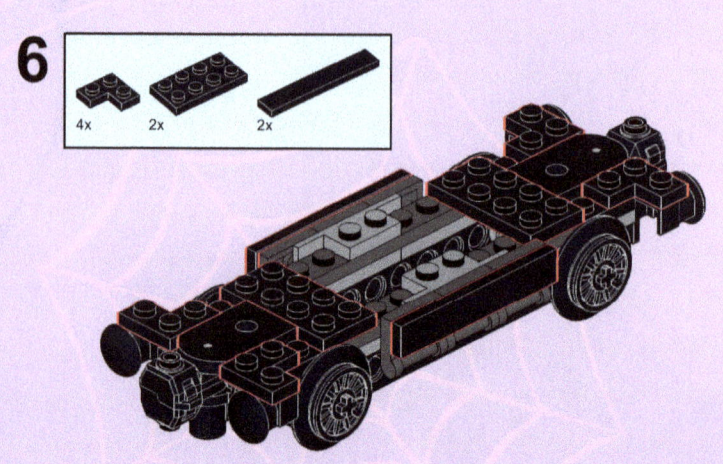

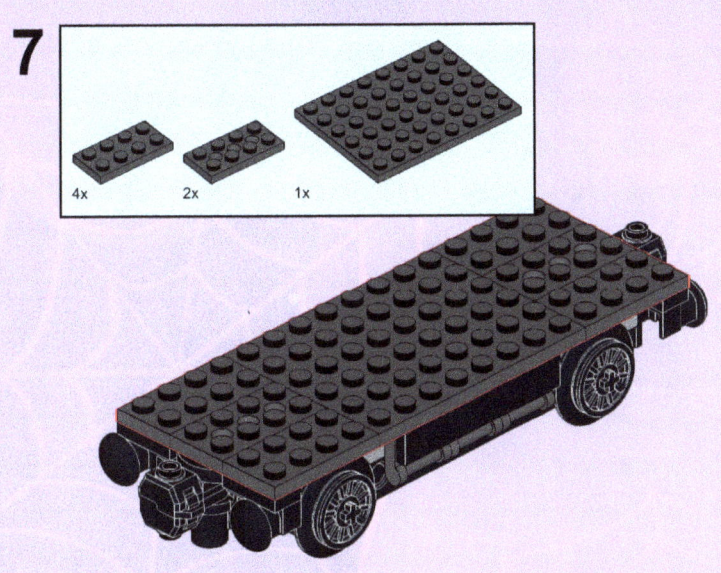
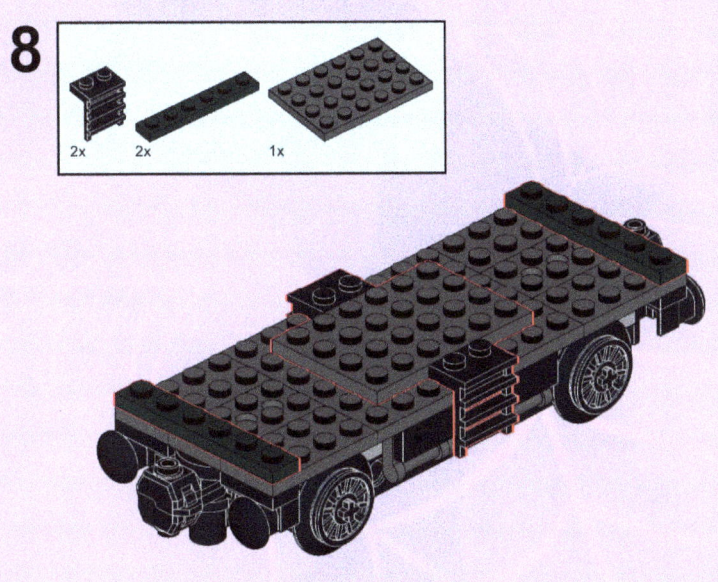

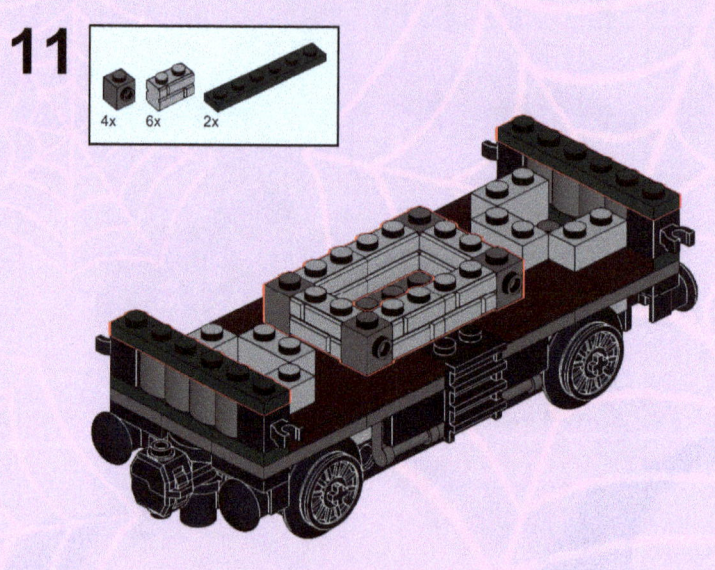

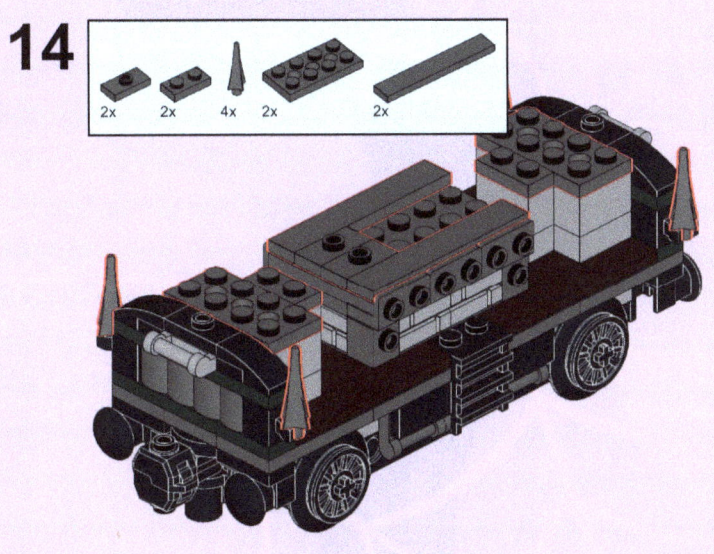
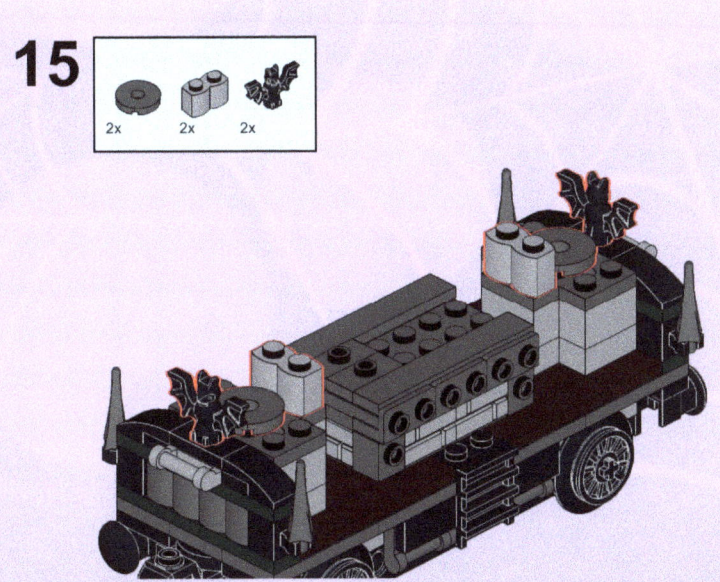

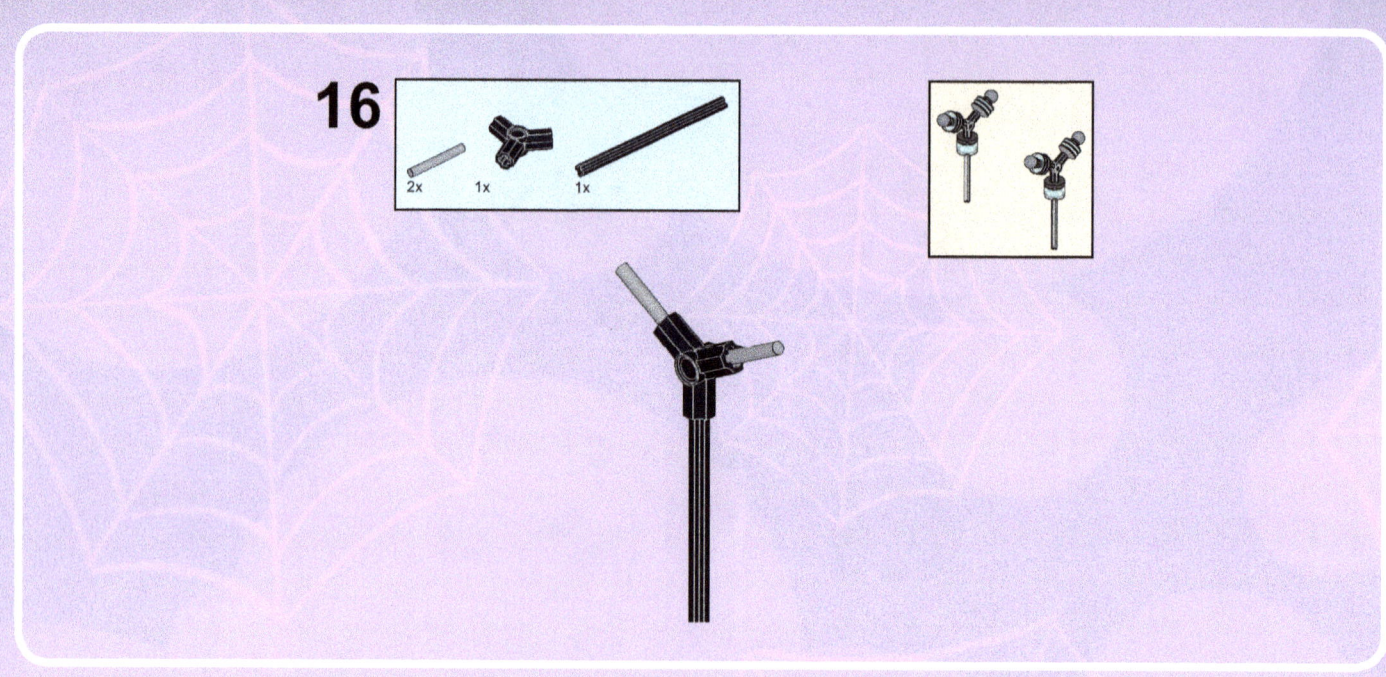
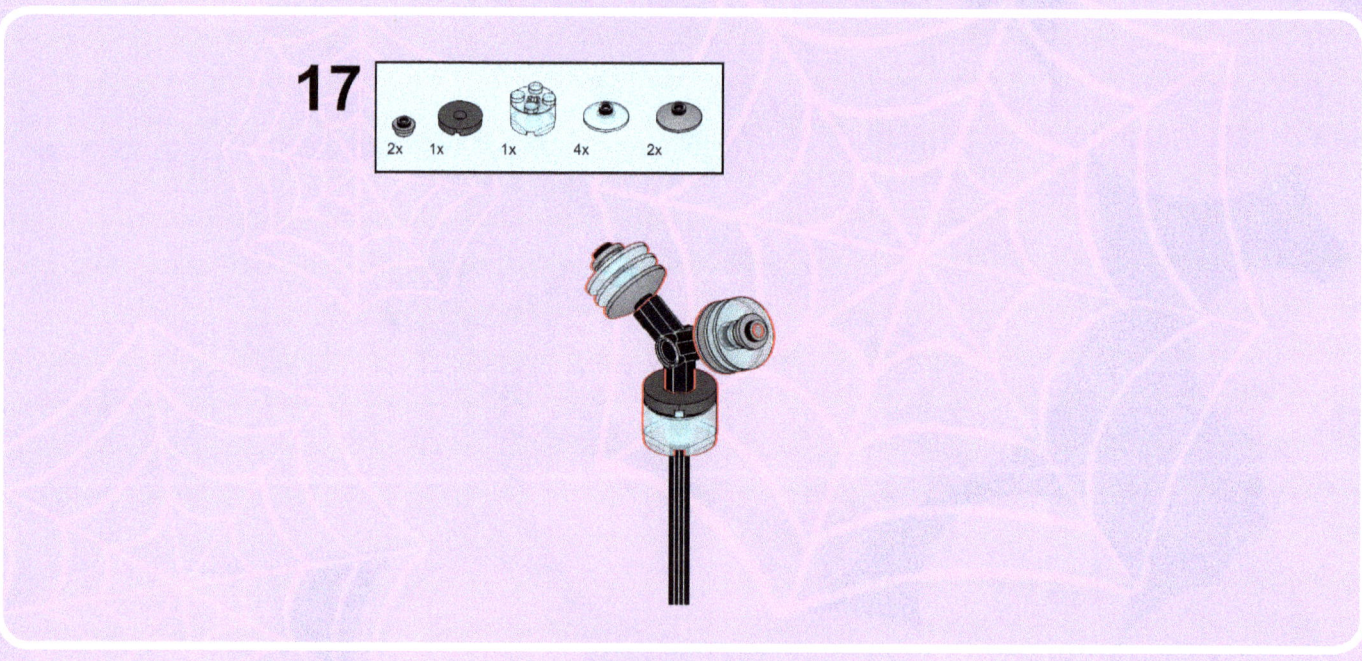
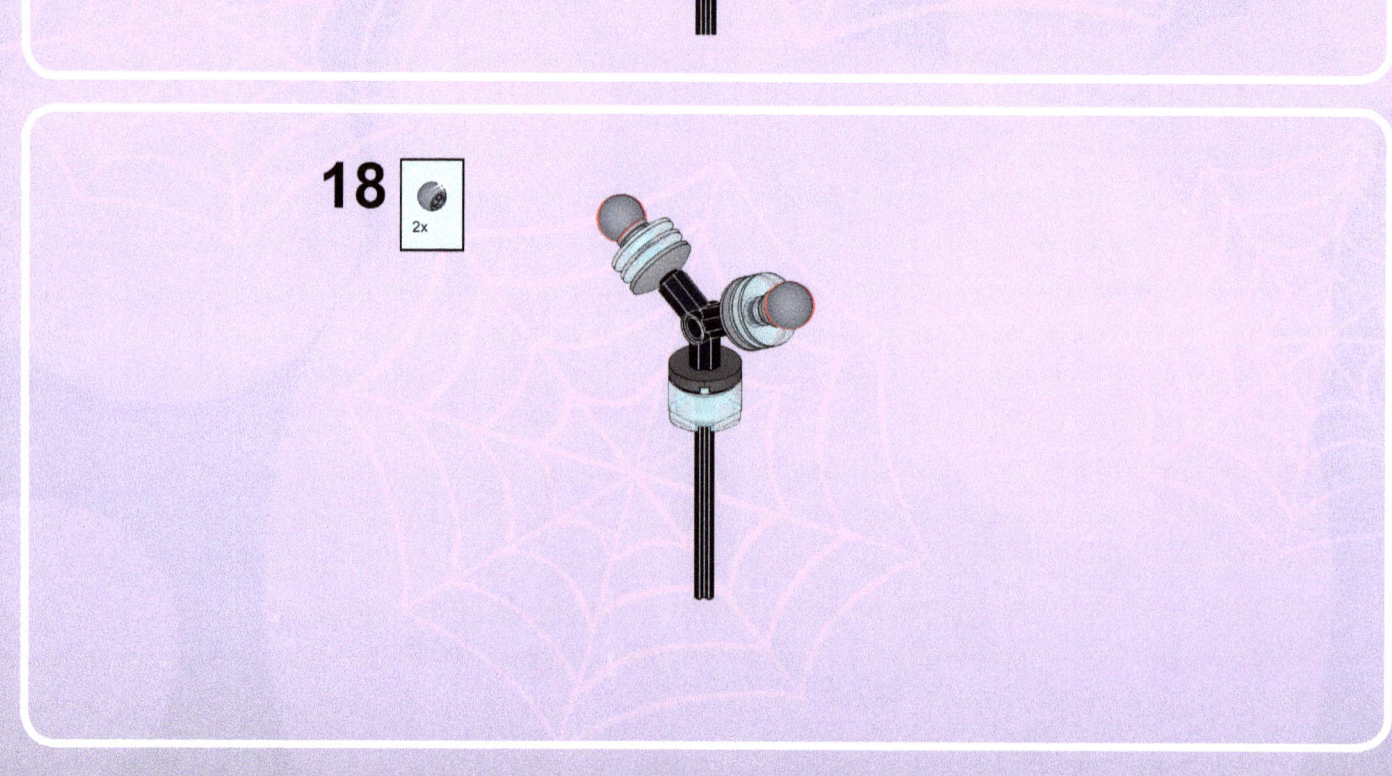

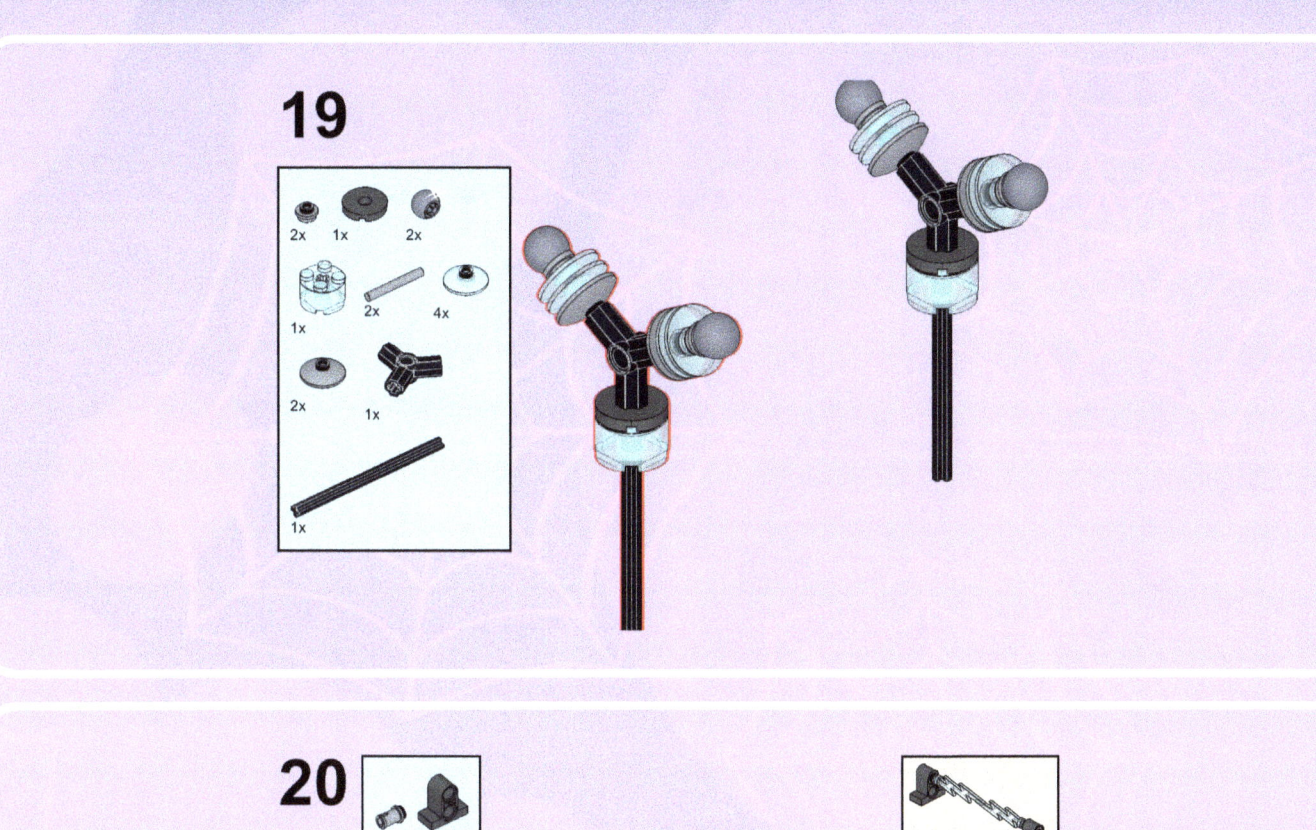
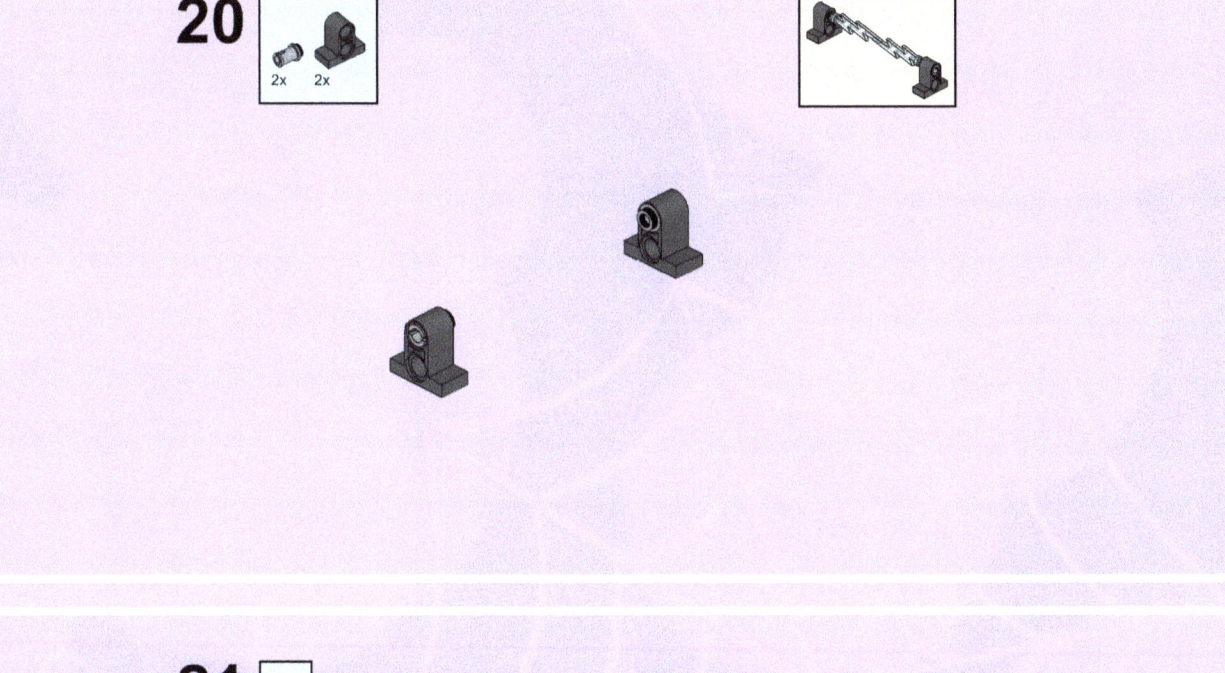
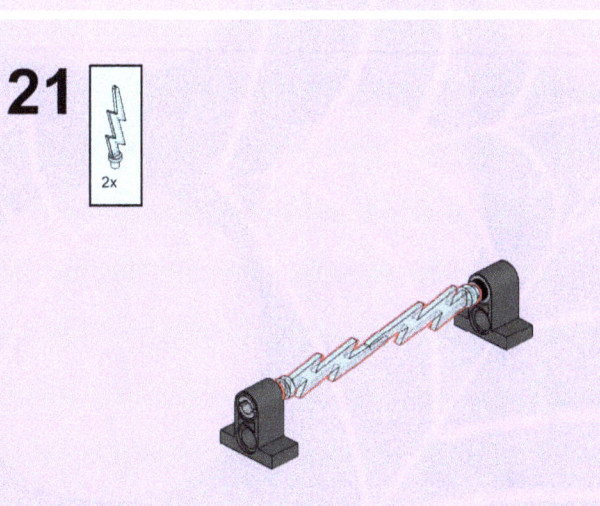

22

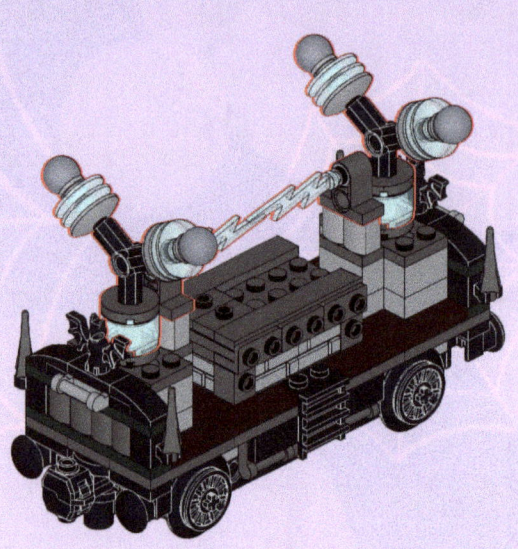

23

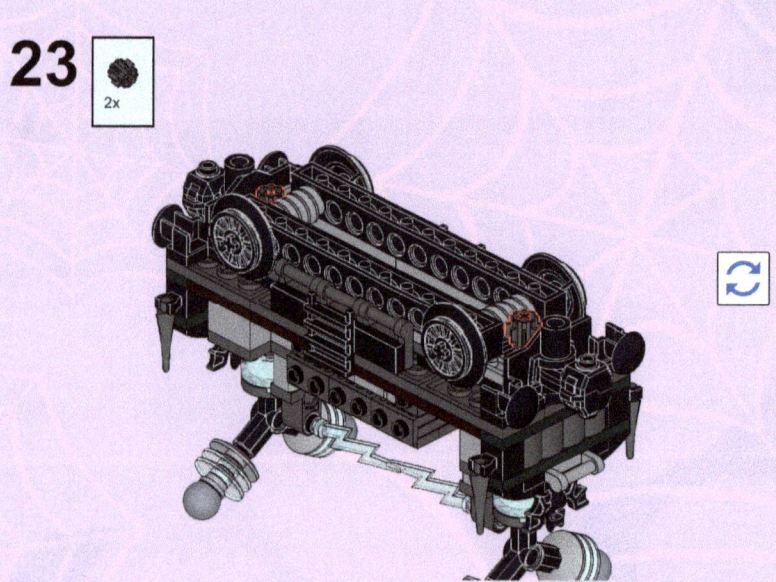

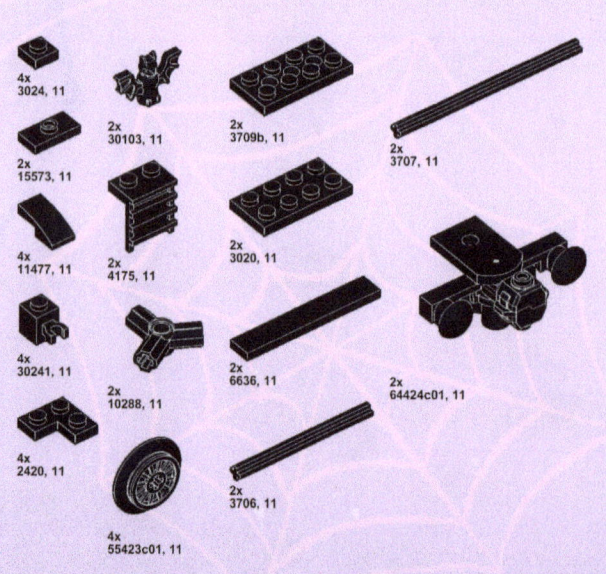

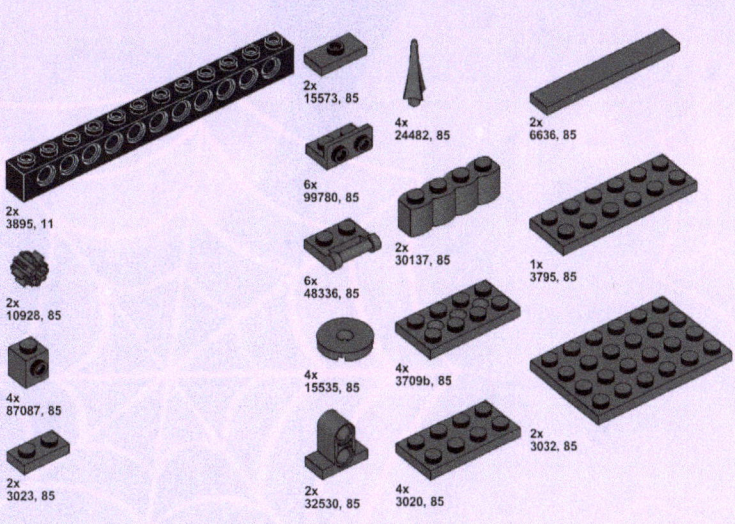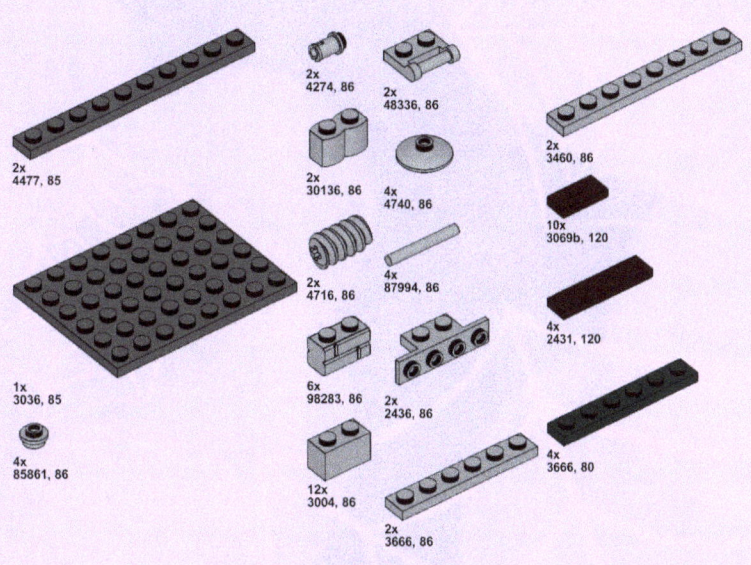

PLANT CAR

Number of bricks: 197
www.inklingbricks.com/parts/plantcar.txt

1
 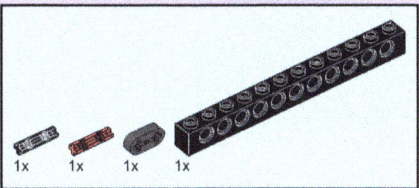
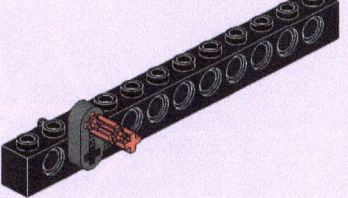

2
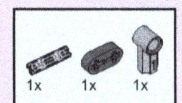
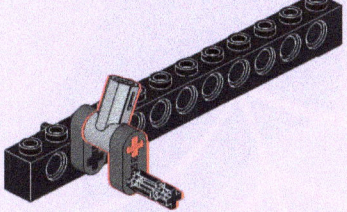

3
 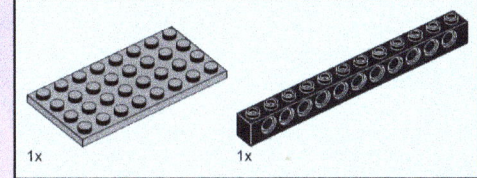

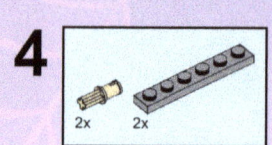

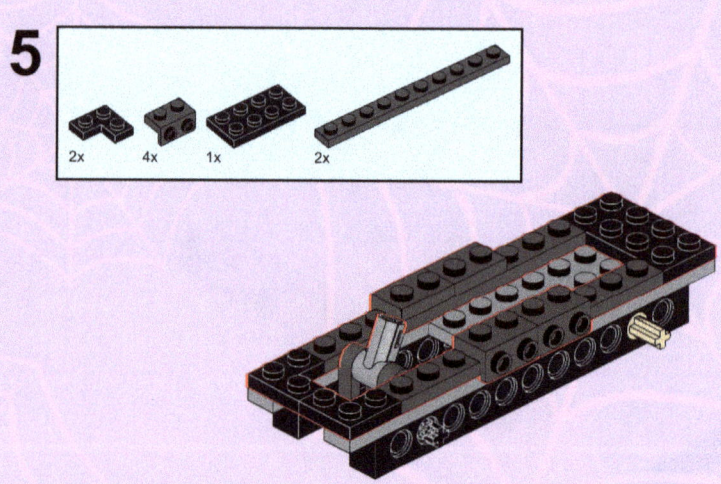

7

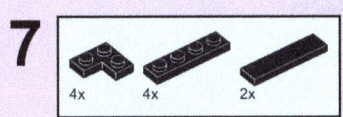

8

9

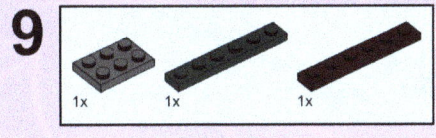

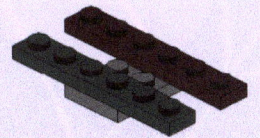

10

11

12

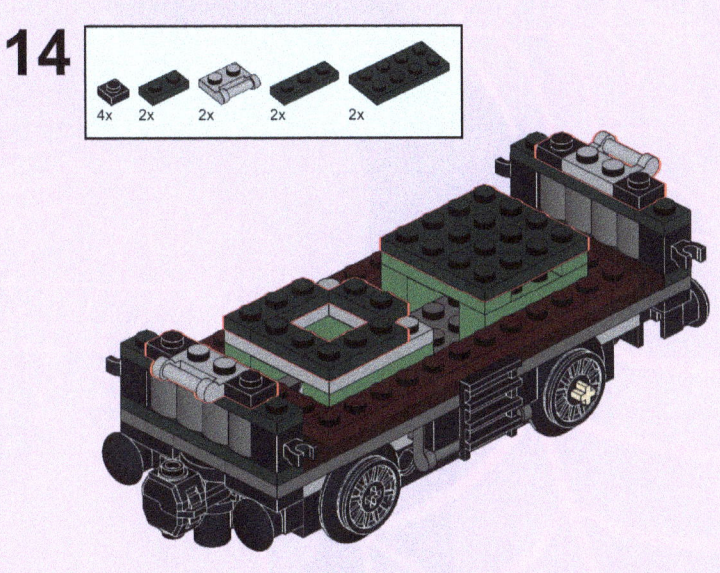
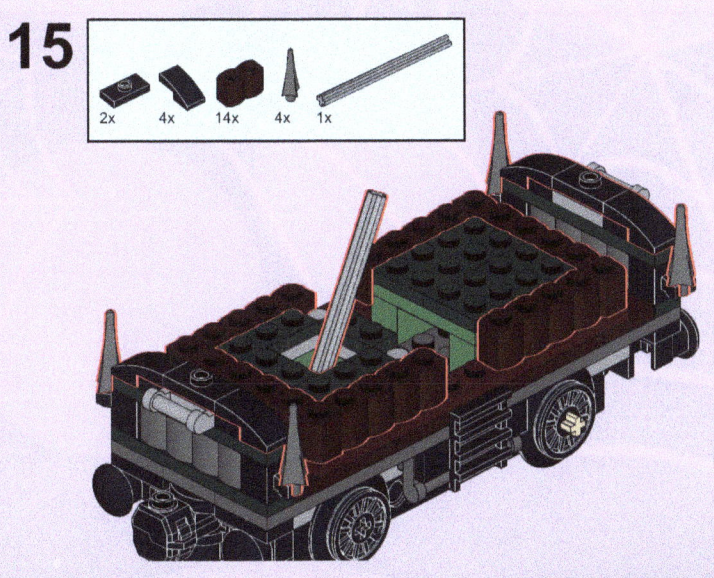

16

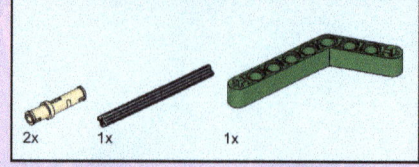 

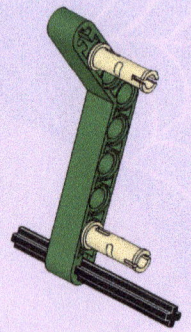

17

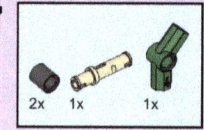

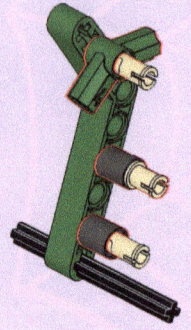

18

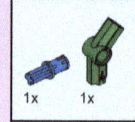 

19

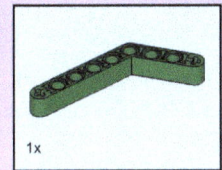
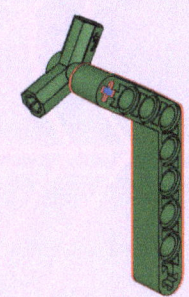

20

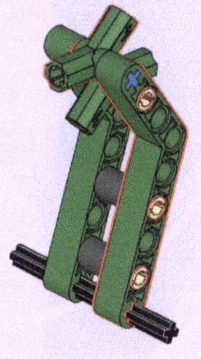

21

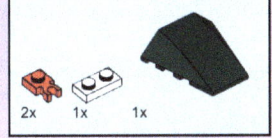
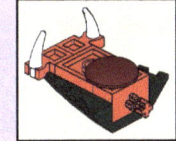

22

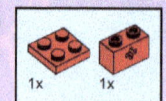

23

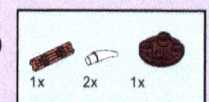

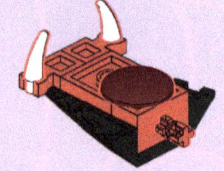

24

25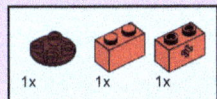

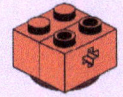

26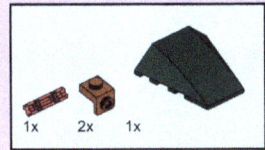

27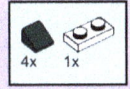

28

29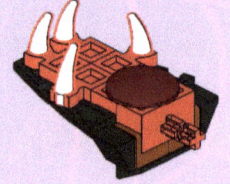

30

31

32

33

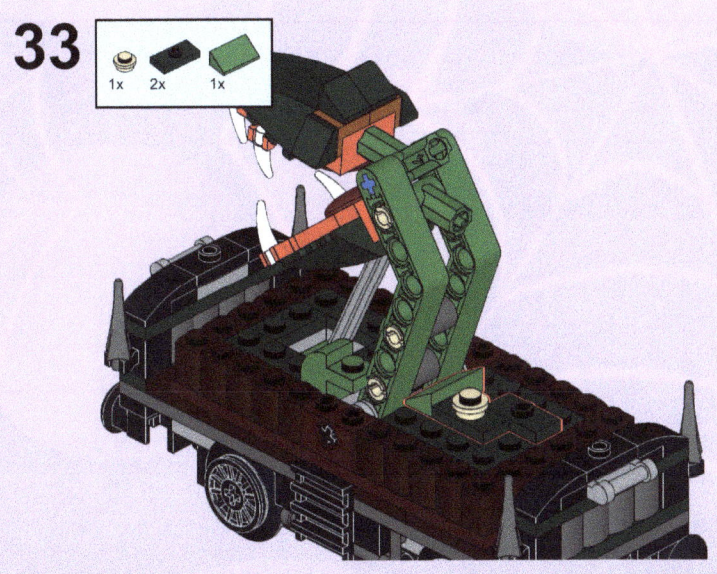

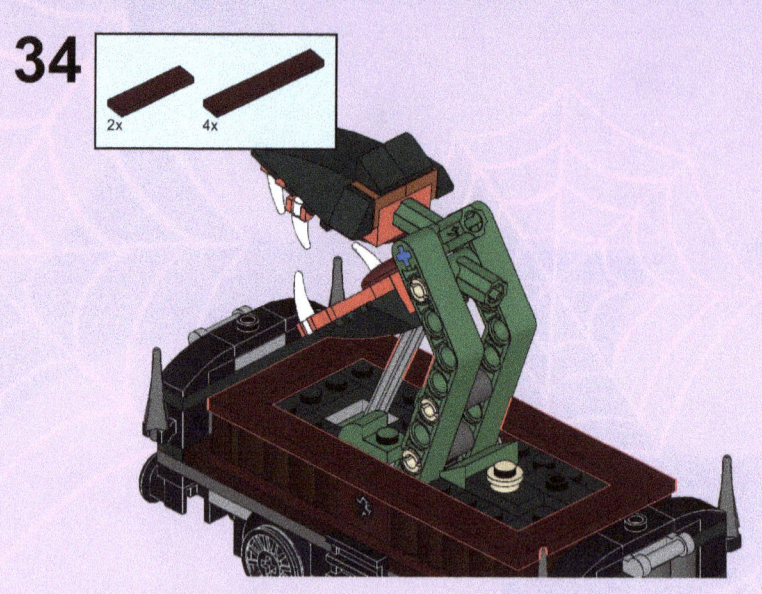
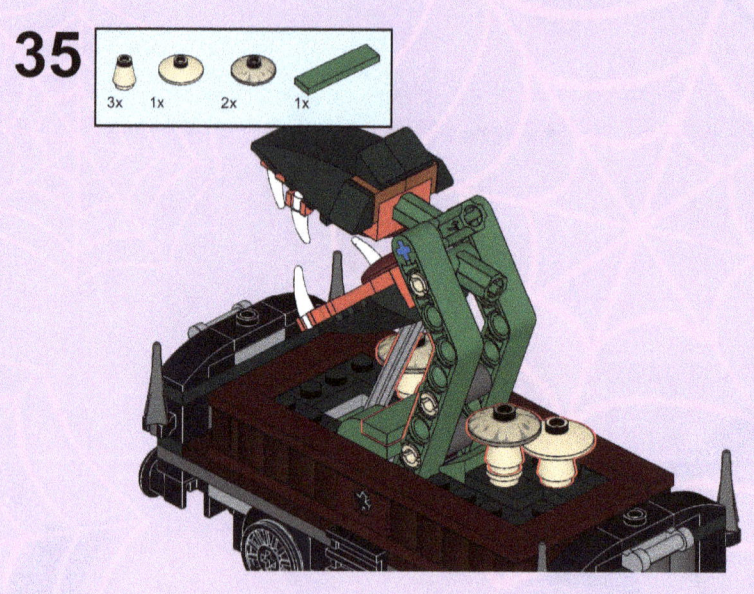

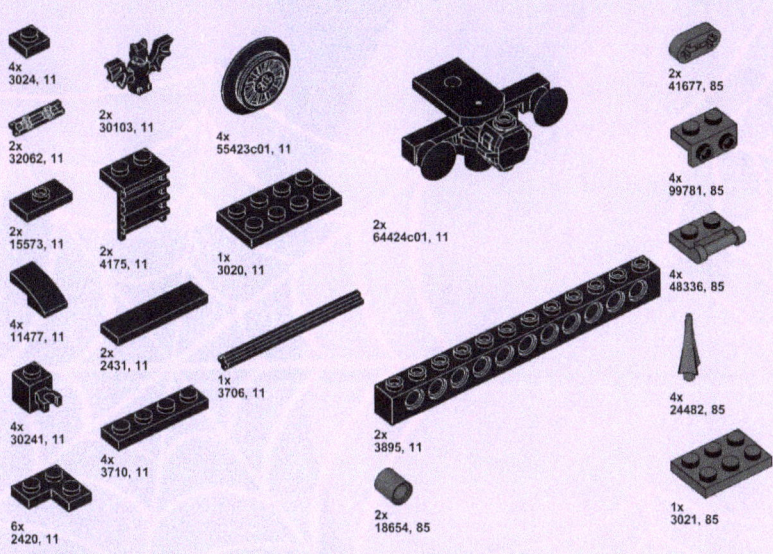
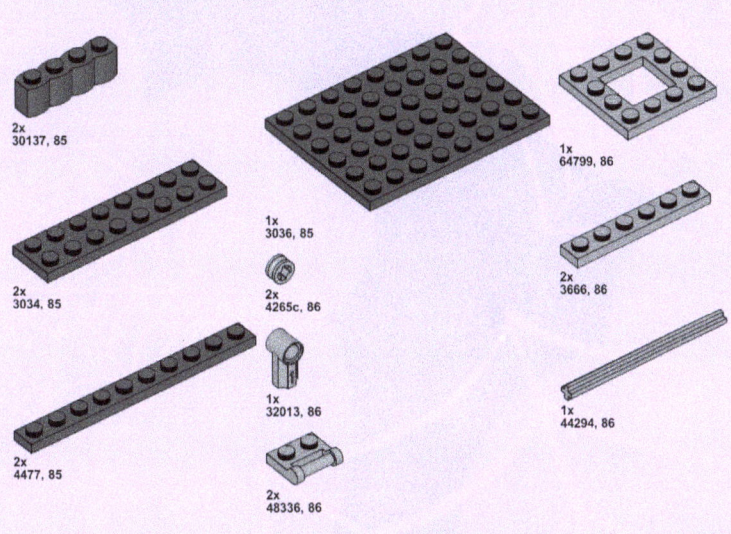
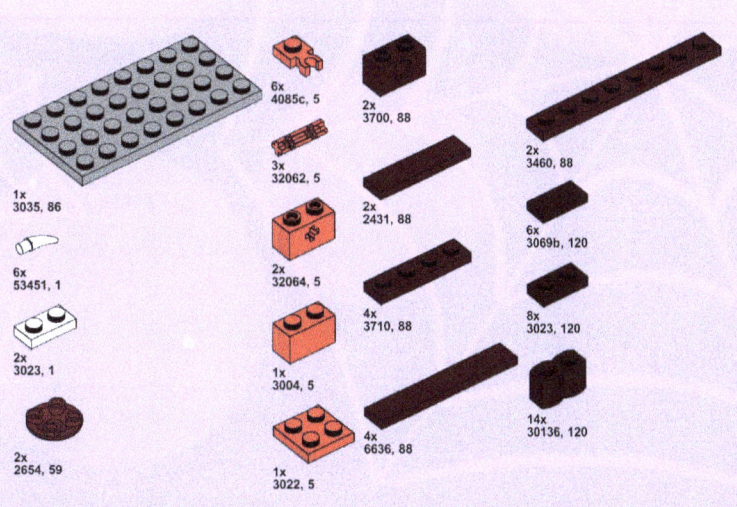

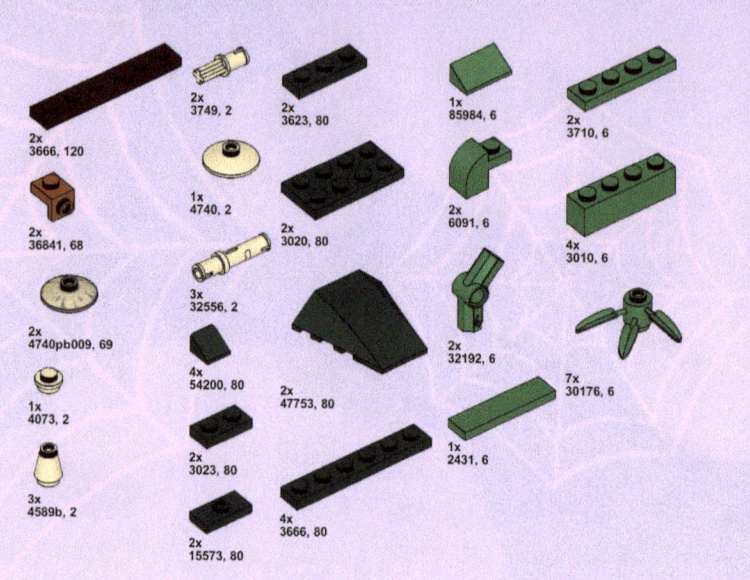

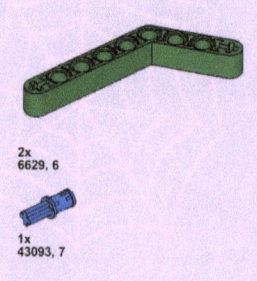

SKELETAL STOCK CAR

Number of bricks: 78
www.inklingbricks.com/parts/skeletalstockcar.txt

1

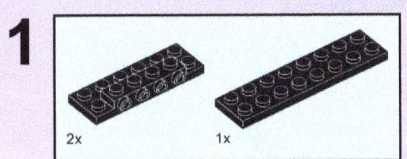

2

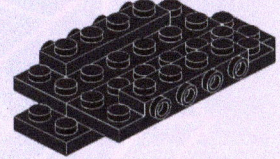

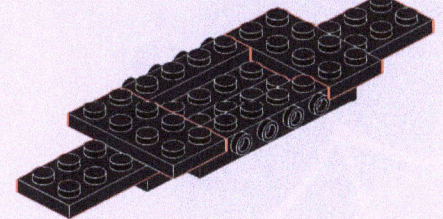

3

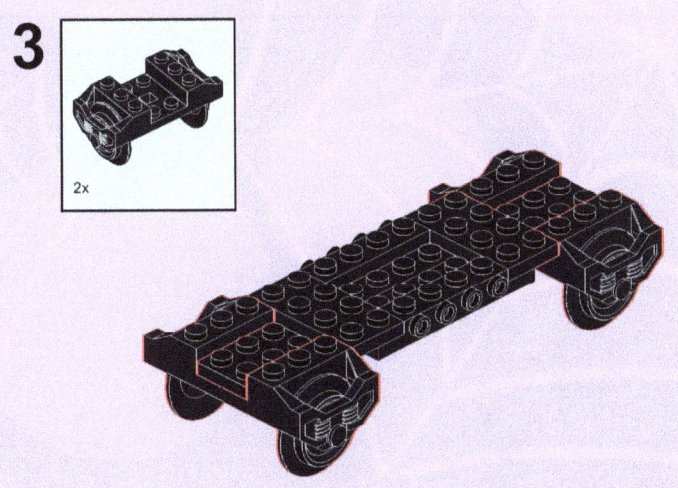

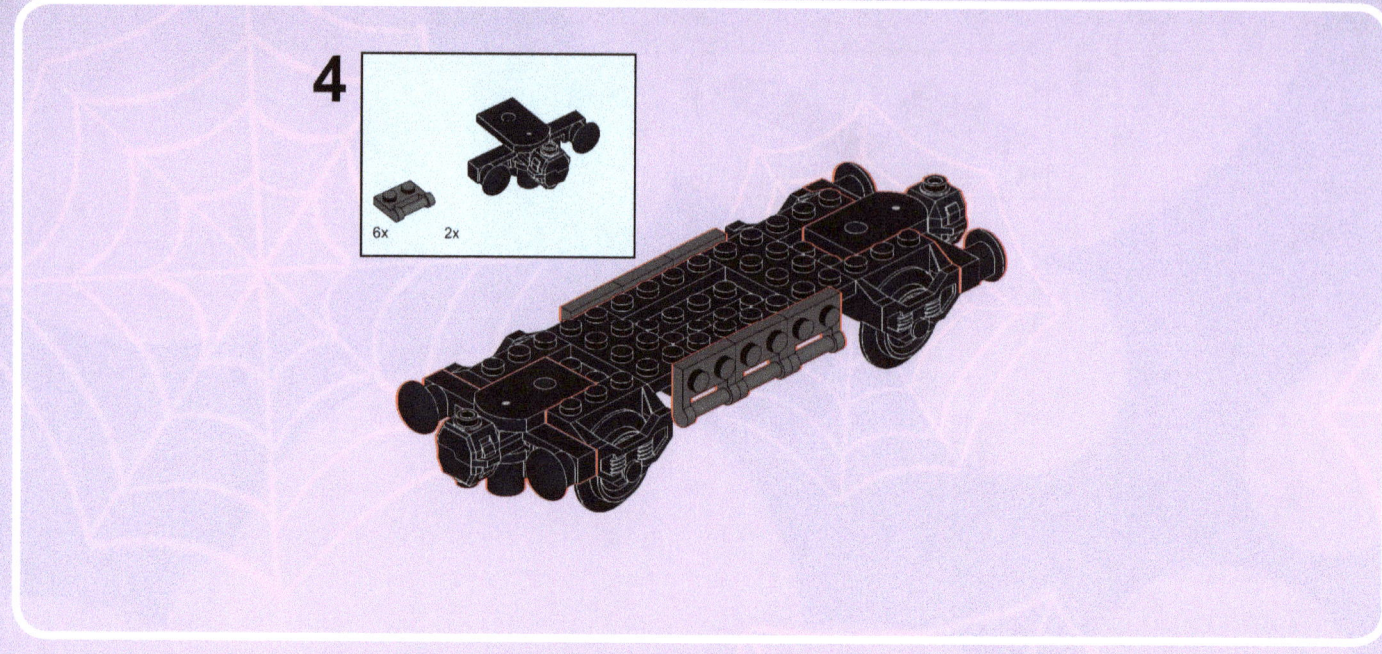

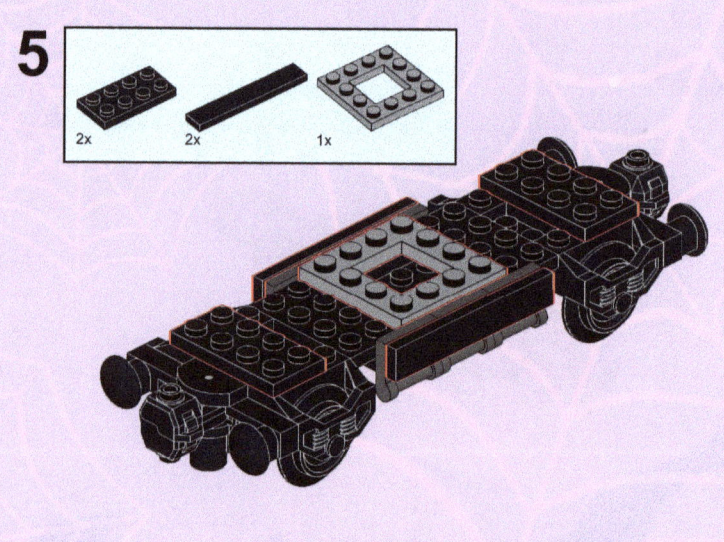

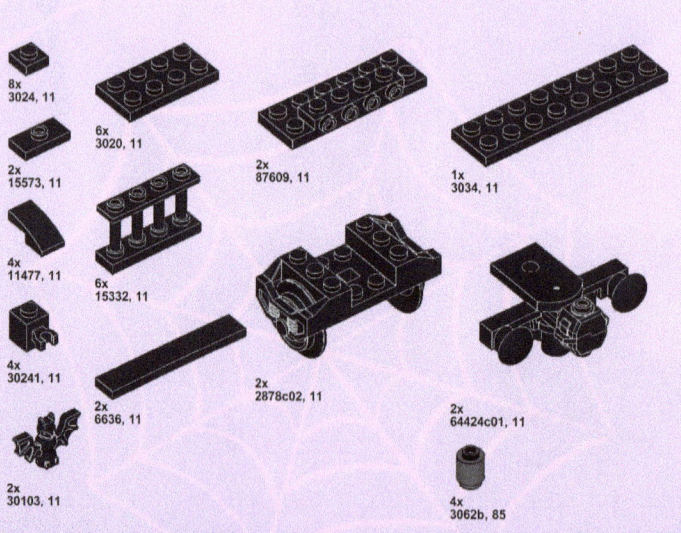

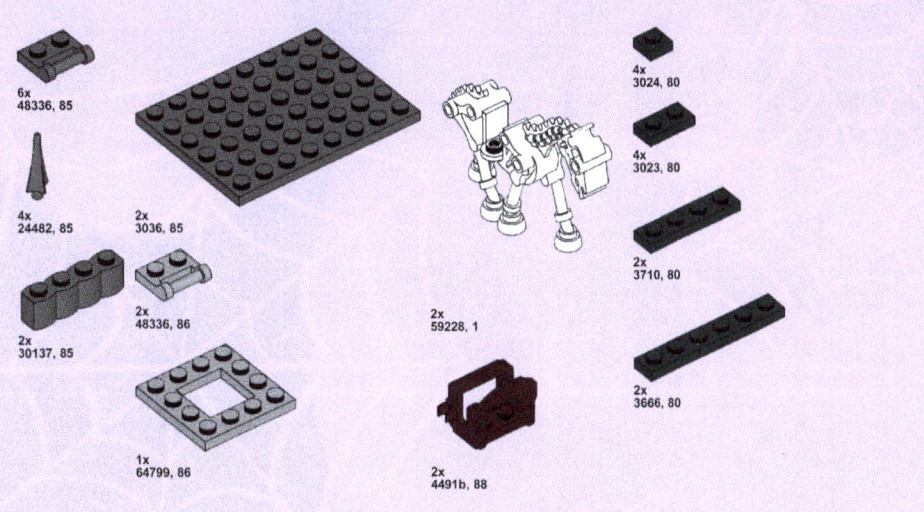

CABOOSE

Number of bricks: 114
www.inklingbricks.com/parts/caboose.txt

1

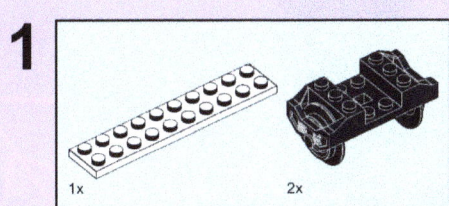

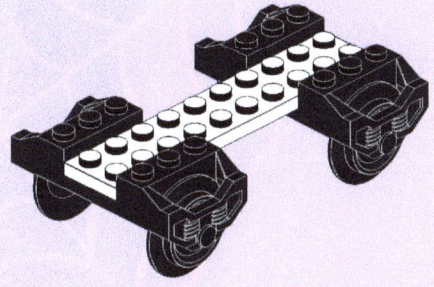

2

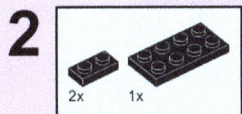
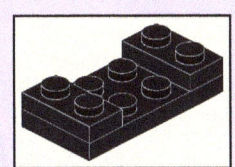

3

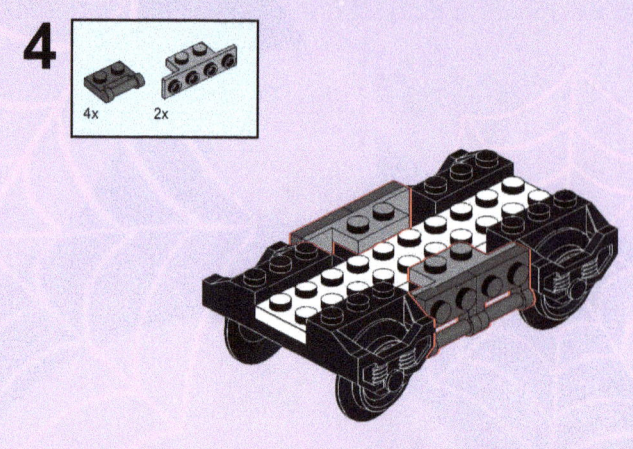
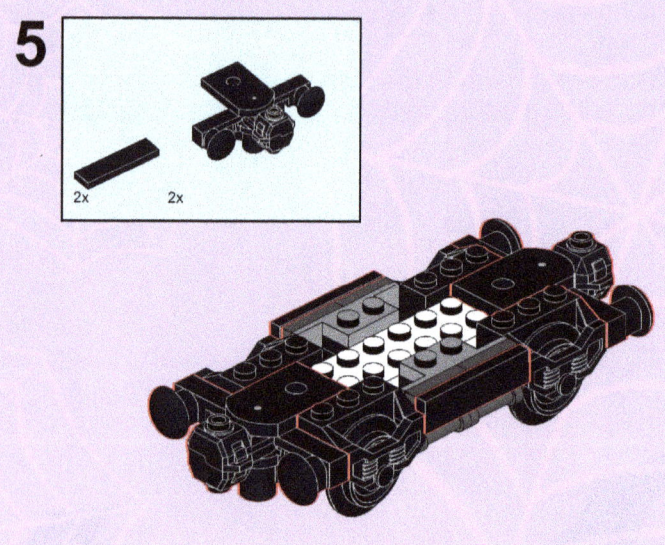
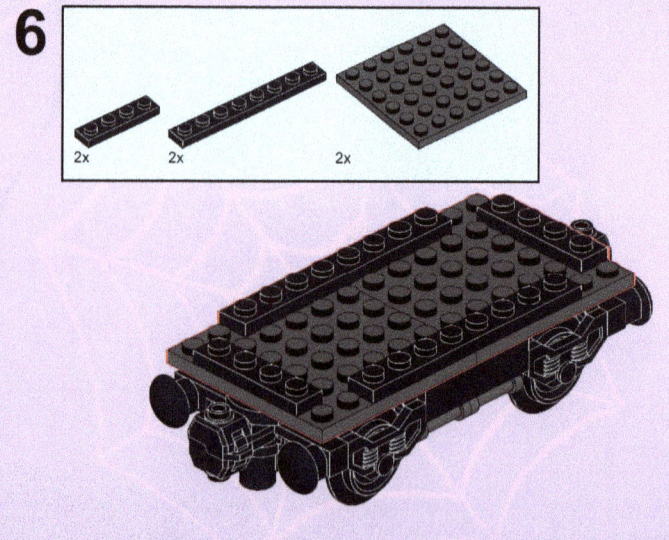

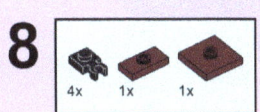

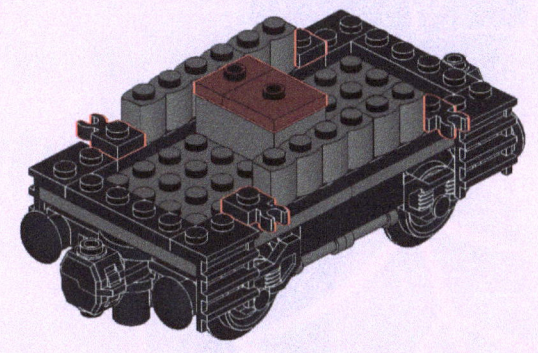

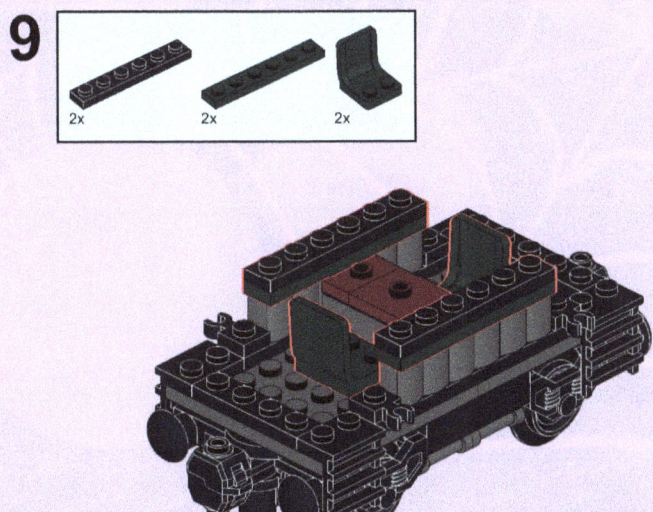

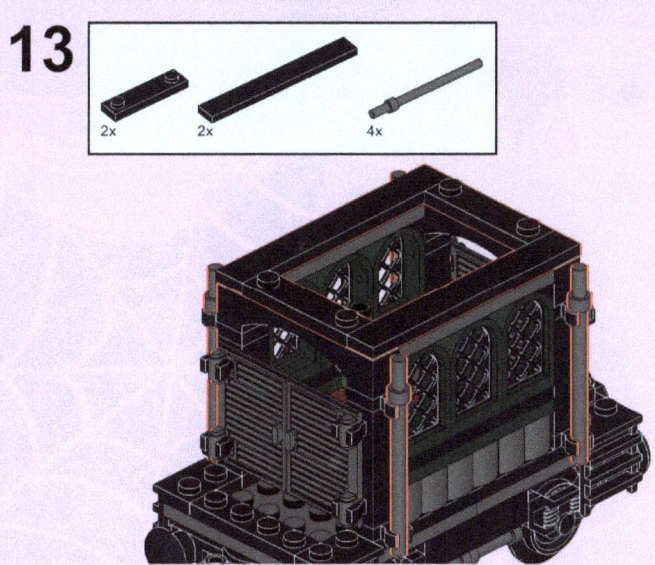
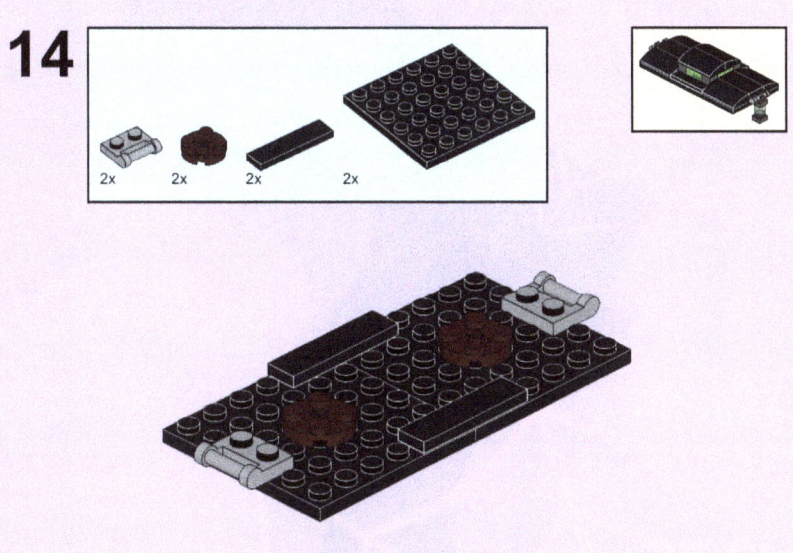
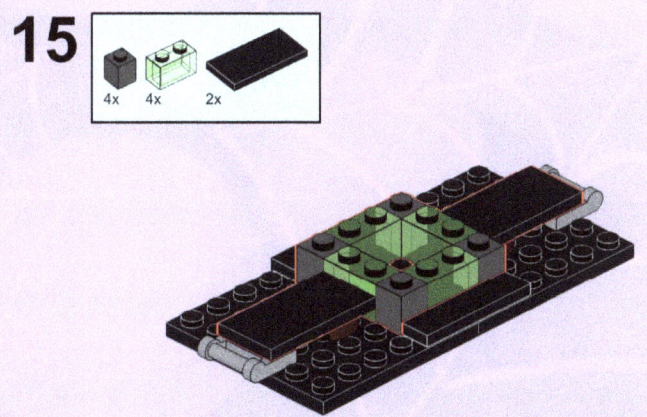

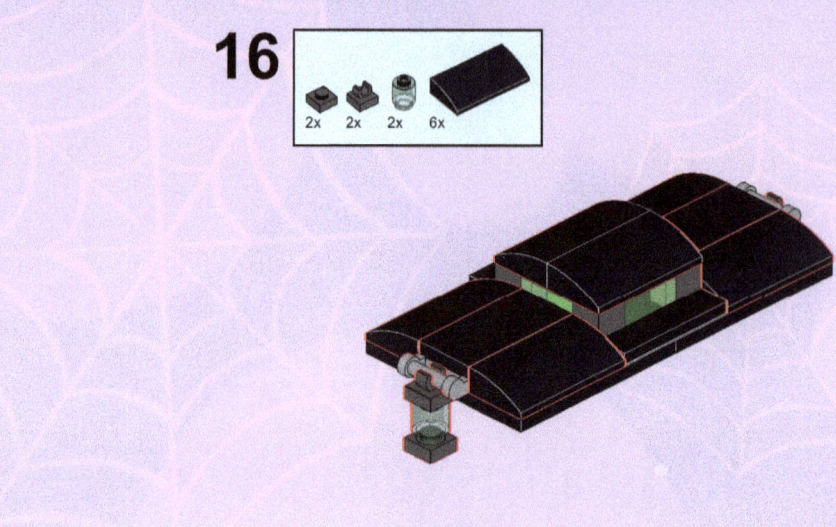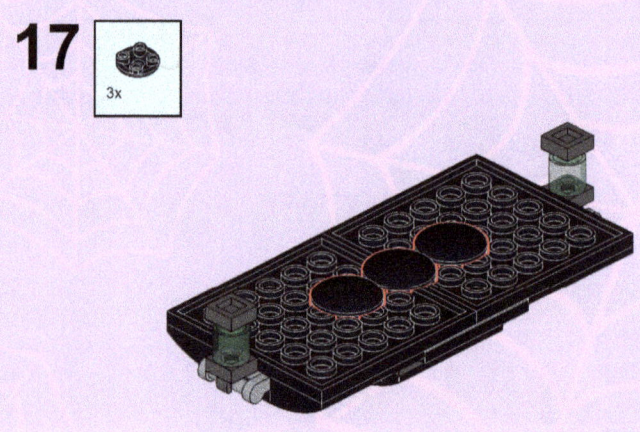

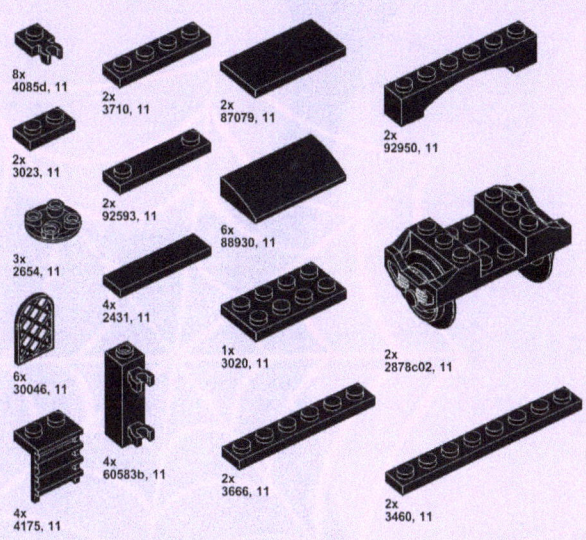
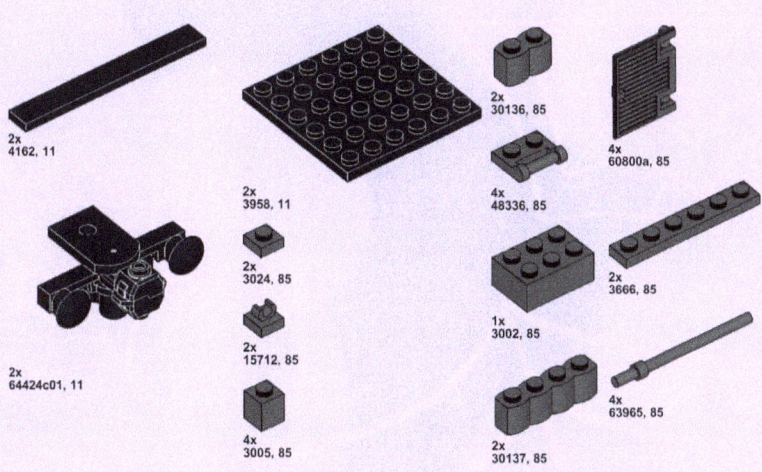
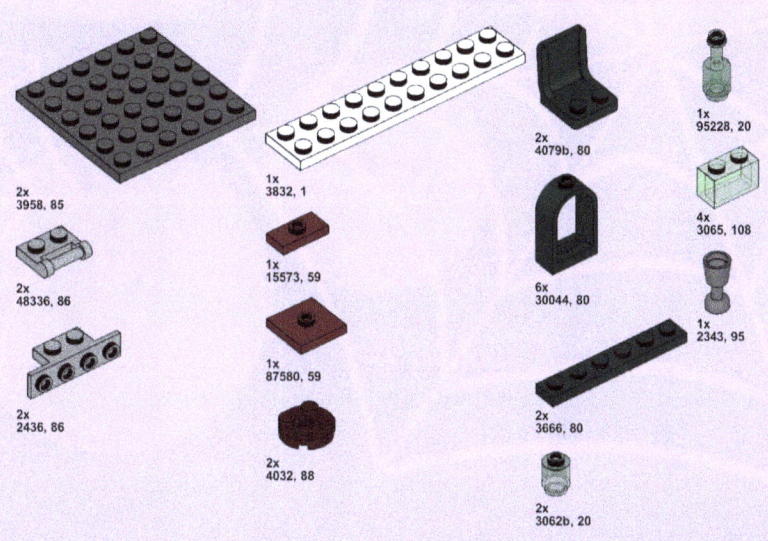

COLLECT THE FULL SERIES!

CHRISTMAS TOWN

CHRISTMAS TRAIN

CHRISTMAS TRAIN 2

CHRISTMAS MOUNTAIN

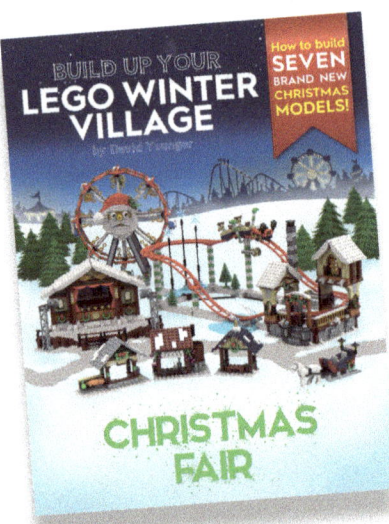
CHRISTMAS FAIR

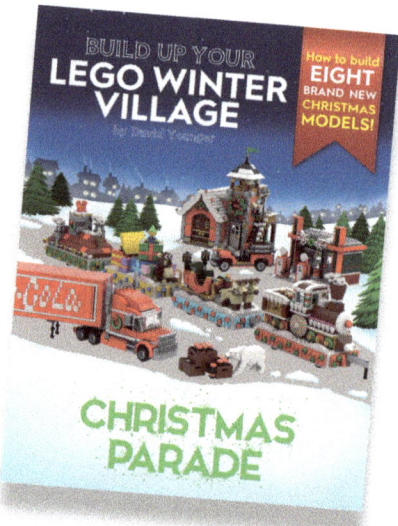
CHRISTMAS PARADE

CHRISTMAS STORIES

CHRISTMAS MEGAFIGURES

HALLOWEEN TRAIN

Available at www.inklingbricks.com

www.ingramcontent.com/pod-product-compliance
Lightning Source LLC
Chambersburg PA
CBHW051247110526
44588CB00025B/2910